# THE TOP NINJA FOODI DUAL AIR FRY OVEN COOKBOOK

**1200 Simpler & Crispier Air Crisp, Broil, Roast, Bake, Toast & More Recipes For Anyone.**

**BY**
**David Burrows**

ISBN: 978-1-63810-099-7

COPYRIGHT © 2022 by David Burrows

All rights reserved. This book is copyright protected and it's for personal use only. Without the prior written permission of the publisher, no part of this publication should be reproduced, distributed, or transmitted in any form or by any means, including photocopying, recording, or other electronic or mechanical methods.

This publication is sold with the idea that the publisher is not required to render accounting, officially permitted, or otherwise, qualified services. If advice is required, it is necessary to seek the services of a legal or professional, a practiced individual in the profession. This document is geared towards providing substantial and reliable information in regard to the topics covered.

**DISCLAIMER**

The information written in this book is for educational and entertainment purposes only. Strenuous efforts have been made to provide accurate, up to date and reliable complete information. The information in this book is true and complete to the best of our knowledge. All recommendations are made without guarantee on the part of the author and publisher.

Neither the publisher nor the author takes any responsibility for any possible consequences of reading or enjoying the recipes in this book. The author and publisher disclaim any liability in connection with the use of information contained in this book. Under no circumstance will any legal responsibility or blame be apportioned against the author or publisher for any reparation, damages, or monetary loss due to the information herein, either directly or indirectly.

Table of Contents

# Introduction .......................................................................................... 10
## Basics of Ninja Foodi Dual Heat Air Fry Oven ............................... 11
### Meaning of Ninja Foodi Dual Heat Air Fry Oven? ................................. 11
## Why You'll Need Ninja Foodi Dual Heat Air Fry Oven ..................... 11
## Steps to Using the Dual Heat Function: ........................................... 11
## Ninja Foodi Dual Air Fry Oven Parts & Accessories ....................... 12
## How to Get Your Air Fryer Oven Ready for First Time Use ............ 12
## Function / Buttons of the Ninja Foodi Dual Heat Air Fry Oven ...... 13
## How to Keep It Clean & Well-Maintained ........................................ 14
## How to Use the Ninja Foodi Dual Heat Air Fry Oven ...................... 14
## Chapter 1: Breakfast ............................................................................ 16
### Savory Parsley Soufflé ............................................................................. 16
### Puffed Egg Tarts ........................................................................................ 17
### Potato & Corned Beef Casserole .............................................................. 18
### Broiled Bacon ............................................................................................ 20
### Banana Bread ............................................................................................ 21
### Breakfast Potatoes .................................................................................... 23
### Sausage Patties ........................................................................................ 24
### French Toast ............................................................................................. 25
### Hard Boiled Eggs ...................................................................................... 26
### Breakfast Pizzas with Muffins .................................................................. 27
### Breakfast Casserole .................................................................................. 28
### Hash Browns ............................................................................................. 29
### Date Bread ................................................................................................. 30
### Savory Sausage & Beans Muffins ............................................................ 31
### Blueberry-Lemon Scones .......................................................................... 32
### Mushrooms Frittata ................................................................................... 33
### Ham and Cheese Scones .......................................................................... 34

Sweet & Spiced Toasts ............................................................................................... 35

Raisin Bran Muffins .................................................................................................. 36

Egg in Hole ............................................................................................................... 37

Breakfast Bake ......................................................................................................... 38

## Chapter 2: Snacks & Appetizer Recipes ............................................ 39

Roasted Cashews ..................................................................................................... 39

Pasta Chips .............................................................................................................. 40

Fiesta Chicken Fingers ............................................................................................. 41

Bacon-Wrapped Filled Jalapeno .............................................................................. 42

Baked Mozzarella Sticks .......................................................................................... 43

Corn on the Cob ...................................................................................................... 44

Air Fryer Ravioli ....................................................................................................... 45

Zucchini Chips ......................................................................................................... 46

Sweet Potato Fries .................................................................................................. 47

French Toast Bites ................................................................................................... 48

Cauliflower Poppers ................................................................................................ 49

Persimmon Chips .................................................................................................... 50

Carrot Chips ............................................................................................................ 51

Tofu Nuggets ........................................................................................................... 52

Chicken & Parmesan Nuggets ................................................................................. 53

Onion Rings ............................................................................................................. 54

Baked Potatoes ....................................................................................................... 55

Eggplant Fries ......................................................................................................... 56

Potato Chips ........................................................................................................... 57

Avocado Fries ......................................................................................................... 58

## Chapter 3: Vegetables & Slides Recipes ........................................... 59

Wine Braised Mushrooms ....................................................................................... 59

Broccoli Casserole ................................................................................................... 60

Feta and Vegetable Bake ......................................................................................... 61

Vegan Cakes ............................................................................................................ 62

Roast Cauliflower and Broccoli ........................................................................... 63
Fried Tortellini .......................................................................................................... 64
Cauliflower Tots ....................................................................................................... 65
Spicy Potato .............................................................................................................. 66
Roasted Green Beans .............................................................................................. 68
Veggie Rice ................................................................................................................ 69
Stuffed Peppers ........................................................................................................ 71
Eggplant Parmesan ................................................................................................. 72
Vegetable Casserole ................................................................................................ 73
Baked Potato ............................................................................................................. 75
Roasted Vegetables ................................................................................................. 76
Green Tomatoes ....................................................................................................... 77
Brussels Sprouts Gratin .......................................................................................... 78
Broiled Broccoli ........................................................................................................ 80
Cheesy Green Bean Casserole ............................................................................... 81
Blue Cheese Soufflés ............................................................................................... 82
Vegetable Nachos .................................................................................................... 83

## Chapter 4: Fish & Seafood Recipes .................................................... 84

Lobster Tail Casserole ............................................................................................ 84
Baked Sardines with Garlic and Oregano .......................................................... 85
Beer-Battered Fish ................................................................................................... 86
Air Fried Fish Sticks ................................................................................................ 87
Baked Tilapia with Butterfly Crumb Topping ................................................... 88
Fish in Yogurt Marinade ........................................................................................ 89
Rum-Glazed Shrimp ............................................................................................... 90
Garlic Butter Salmon Bites .................................................................................... 91
Tilapia with Herbs and Garlic .............................................................................. 92
Breaded Shrimp ....................................................................................................... 93
Air Fried Fish Cakes ................................................................................................ 94
Lobster Tails with Lemon-Garlic Butter ............................................................. 95

Fish Casserole ........................................................................................................ 96
Scallops with Chanterelles ..................................................................................... 97
Crispy Flounder ..................................................................................................... 98
Prawns in Butter Sauce .......................................................................................... 99
Fish Newburg with Haddock ................................................................................ 100
Seafood Medley Mix ............................................................................................. 101
Buttered Crab Shells ............................................................................................. 102
Scallops with Capers Sauce .................................................................................. 103
Scallops with Spinach ........................................................................................... 104
Shrimp Fajitas ....................................................................................................... 105
Seafood Casserole ................................................................................................ 106
Lemon Pepper Shrimp .......................................................................................... 107
Spicy Bay Scallops ................................................................................................ 108
Maple Bacon Salmon ............................................................................................ 109

## Chapter 5: Poultry Recipes ................................................................. 110

Creamy Chicken Casserole ................................................................................... 110
Duck a la Orange .................................................................................................. 111
Baked Duck ........................................................................................................... 112
Spiced Roasted Chicken ....................................................................................... 113
Spicy Chicken Legs ............................................................................................... 114
Gingered Chicken Drumsticks .............................................................................. 115
Sweet and Spicy Chicken Drumsticks .................................................................. 116
Honey-Glazed Chicken Drumsticks ...................................................................... 117
Sweet and Sour Chicken Thighs ........................................................................... 118
Herb Butter Chicken ............................................................................................. 119
Breaded Chicken Tenderloins ............................................................................... 120
Parmesan Chicken Bake ....................................................................................... 121
Chicken Alfredo Bake ........................................................................................... 122
Marinated Ranch Broiled Chicken ........................................................................ 123
Cheesy Chicken Cutlets ........................................................................................ 124

Lemon-Lime Chicken ................................................................................. 125
Brie Stuffed Chicken Breasts .................................................................... 126
Simple Turkey Breast ................................................................................ 127
Chicken Kabobs ......................................................................................... 128
Oat Crusted Chicken Breasts .................................................................... 129
Roasted Goose ........................................................................................... 130
Crispy Chicken Cutlets .............................................................................. 131
Blackened Chicken Bake ........................................................................... 132
Herbed Duck Breast .................................................................................. 133
Brine-Soaked Turkey ................................................................................. 134
Chicken Kebabs ......................................................................................... 135
Roasted Duck ............................................................................................. 136
Parmesan Chicken Meatballs ................................................................... 137
Chicken and Rice Casserole ..................................................................... 138
Chicken Potato Bake ................................................................................. 139
Spanish Chicken Bake ............................................................................... 140

## Chapter 6: Red Meat Recipes ................................................................ 141
Beef Short Ribs .......................................................................................... 141
Savory Pork Roast ..................................................................................... 142
Czech Roast Pork ...................................................................................... 143
Herby Pork Bake ........................................................................................ 144
Roasted Pork Belly .................................................................................... 145
Baked Beef Stew ........................................................................................ 146
Russian Baked Beef ................................................................................... 147
Lamb Chops ............................................................................................... 148
Lamb and Potato Bake .............................................................................. 149
Ground Beef Casserole ............................................................................. 150
Tarragon Beef Shanks ............................................................................... 151
Garlic Braised Ribs .................................................................................... 152
Beef Zucchini Shashliks ............................................................................ 153

Mint Lamb with Toasted Hazelnuts ................................................................. 154
Lamb Chops with Rosemary Sauce .................................................................. 155
Garlicky Lamb Chops ........................................................................................ 156
Lamb Kebabs ..................................................................................................... 157
Lamb Rack with Lemon Crust .......................................................................... 158
Greek lamb Farfalle ........................................................................................... 159
New York Strip Steak ........................................................................................ 160
Minced Lamb Casserole .................................................................................... 161
Za'atar Chops ..................................................................................................... 162
Pork Chops with Cashew Sauce ....................................................................... 163
American Roast Beef ........................................................................................ 164
Roast Beef and Yorkshire Pudding .................................................................. 165
Baked Pork Chops ............................................................................................. 166

## Chapter 7: Dessert Recipes ............................................................... 167

Caramel Apple Pie ............................................................................................. 167
Peanut Brittle Bars ............................................................................................ 168
Cherry Jam tarts ................................................................................................ 169
Cookie Cake ....................................................................................................... 171
Fried Oreo .......................................................................................................... 172
Chocolate Chip Cookies .................................................................................... 173
Banana Pancakes Dippers ................................................................................ 174
Cinnamon Rolls ................................................................................................. 175
Blueberry Hand Pies ......................................................................................... 176
Broiled Bananas with Cream ............................................................................ 177
Roasted Bananas ............................................................................................... 178
Chocolate Oatmeal Cookies .............................................................................. 179
Cherry Clafoutis ................................................................................................ 180
Vanilla Soufflé ................................................................................................... 181
Fudge Brownies ................................................................................................. 183
Nutella Banana Muffins .................................................................................... 184

Air Fried Churros ................................................................................................. 185
Air Fried Doughnuts ............................................................................................ 186
Cannoli ................................................................................................................... 187

# Introduction

There are two modes on the Ninja Foodi Dual Heat Air Fry Oven: Dual Heat Mode and Air Oven Mode. Sear Crisp, Rapid Bake, Griddle, Fresh Pizza, and Frozen Pizza are the five cooking capabilities available in the Dual Heat Mode. Air Fry, Air Roast, Bake, Broil, Toast, Reheat, Dehydrate, and Bagel are the eight cooking functions available in the Air Oven Mode. This cooking device is a multipurpose cookware with a small footprint.

It is equipped with dual-heat technology. With 500°F direct contact heat and quick airflow, you can sear and crisp thick-cut steak and prepare delicious meals in this multifunctional oven.

An Air Fry Basket, Wire Rack, Removable Crumb Tray, and SearPlate are included with the Ninja Foodi Dual Heat Air Fry Oven. The Air Fry Basket is used for both air frying and dehydrating. If using other oven accessories, slot the Wire Rack into the bottom rails for the Reheat, Broil, and Bake cooking capabilities.

SearPlate is utilised for cooking tasks such as Fresh Pizza, Frozen Pizza, Sear Crisp, Rapid Bake, Broil, Griddle, Air Roast, and Bake.

Your most delectable and appetising recipes are included in the cookbook, along with thorough and clear instructions. Select your favourite recipe and begin cooking with your preferred cooking method. This book has a wide range of recipes, from breakfast to dessert. It cooks food with minimal fats and oils. With this gadget, you will be able to prepare healthy and delicious meals on a daily basis. This cookbook and your Ninja Foodi Dual Heat Air Fry Oven are essential cooking appliance and are sufficient for your kitchen, and you won't need to buy another appliance because it has all the characteristics you'll ever need.

# Basics of Ninja Foodi Dual Heat Air Fry Oven

## Meaning of Ninja Foodi Dual Heat Air Fry Oven?

The Ninja Foodi Dual Heat Air Fry Oven features dual technology, 13 cooking options, 4 detachable parts, and 12 control buttons. It uses dual technology, in which sear plates are directly heated to 500°F and your meal is crisped by quick air at the same time. It cooks air fryers 65 percent faster than other ovens. It has a large enough capacity to feed your entire family.

There are two modes on the Ninja Foodi Dual Heat Air Fry Oven: Frozen Pizza, Fresh Pizza, Griddle, Rapid Bake, and Sear Crisp cooking capabilities are available in dual heat mode. Air Fry, Air Roast, Dehydrate, Reheat, Bake, Toast, Broil, and Bagel cooking operations are available in the Air Oven mode. These essential cooking functions are sufficient for your kitchen, and you won't need to buy another appliance because it has all the characteristics you'll ever need. The cleaning procedure for this device is simple.

## Why You'll Need Ninja Foodi Dual Heat Air Fry Oven

**Quick Cooking:**
Food cooks faster in the Ninja Foodi Dual Heat Air Fry Oven than in a standard oven.

**Tasty & Healthier Meals:**
You should use the Ninja Foodi Dual Heat Air Fry Oven if you want to eat healthy dishes because it consumes fewer oils and fats than other machines. It remains among the best methods of cooking healthier foods because it uses fewer oils or fats.

**Multi-Functionality:**
The Ninja Foodi Dual Heat Air Fry Oven features 13 culinary capabilities in one appliance. Sear Crisp, Rapid Bake, Griddle, Fresh Pizza, and Frozen Pizza, as well as Air fry, Air Roast, Bake, Broil, Toast, Reheat, Dehydrate, and Bagel, are all included. You won't need to buy any other appliances because you'll have access to all of the cooking tasks you'll need on a daily basis.

## Steps to Using the Dual Heat Function:

There are five cooking functions available in this dual heat mode: Sear crisp, rapid bake, griddle, fresh pizza, frozen pizza, and so on. These cooking functions are performed using SearPlate. SearPlate functions similarly to a cast iron pan.

- ❖ Add the SearPlate in the bottom of the Ninja Food Dual Oven and click the Power function on the appliance.
- ❖ Next, select the DUAL HEAT MODE function while pressing and holding the START/STOP button.
- ❖ To alter the cooking time, press the TIME/SLICES button and rotate the dial. Press the TIME/SLICES button one more to modify the cooking time. To alter the temperature, press the TEMP/SHADE button and twist the dial.

- ❖ To begin preheating, push the START/STOP button. It will take 5 to 10 minutes to pre-heat the oven. When the preheating time is up, the display will notify you.
- ❖ Once the SearPlate and oven are preheated, the timer starts counting down. Turn the dial to raise or reduce cooking time while it's cooking. To turn off the pot, turn the dial.

## Ninja Foodi Dual Air Fry Oven Parts & Accessories

Air Fryer Basket, Wire Rack, SearPlate, and Removable Crumb Tray come standard with the Ninja Foodi Dual Heat Air Fry Oven.

**SEARPLATE:** Broil, Rapid Bake, Bake, Air Roast, Griddle, Fresh Pizza, Frozen Pizza, and Sear Crisp are all done on the SearPlate. SearPlate is simple to clean. In the Ninja Foodi Dual Heat Air Fry Oven, place the SearPlate.

**REMOVABLE CRUMB TRAY:** Always position a Removable Crumb Tray below the bottom heating element. It can only be washed with your hands.

**AIR FRYER BASKET:** An Air Fryer Basket is used for dehydrating and air frying. For storage, slide the Air Fryer Basket into the Ninja Foodi Dual Heat Air Fry Oven's top rails. The Air Fryer Basket is simple to clean. Fill the Air Fry Basket halfway with food and place it in the unit.

**WIRE RACK:** The Wire Rack can be used for cooking bagel and toast. In the Ninja Foodi Dual Heat Air Fry Oven, place the Wire Rack. The Wire Rack is simple to clean. For storing, place in the bottom of the Ninja Foodi Dual Heat Air Fry Oven. Reheat any over-oven accessories by sliding them into the bottom rails.

## How to Get Your Air Fryer Oven Ready for First Time Use

There are a few things you should do to prepare your appliance for usage before utilising it. They include:

- ❖ Remove all labelling, papers, tapes, and marketing materials when you receive your appliance.
- ❖ Take all parts and accessories from their box. To avoid injury, hazard, and risk, read the instructional manual, including the operational guidance to avoid property damage.
- ❖ Using a non-abrasive sponge, properly clean the parts and accessories in warm soapy water.
- ❖ Wash the SearPlate with warm soapy water and dry completely with a non-abrasive sponge.
- ❖ Insert all of the accessories in the oven after they've dried completely. Turn the dial to air fry and press the Air Oven Mode button.

- ❖ Use the dial to select 20 minutes by pressing the time function.
- ❖ Turn the dial to 450°F after pressing the temperature function.
- ❖ Now you may utilise the Air Fry Oven.

## Function / Buttons of the Ninja Foodi Dual Heat Air Fry Oven

There are 13 cooking functions on the Ninja Foodi Dual Heat Air Fry Oven. The following culinary functions are described in detail:

**AIR ROAST FUNCTION:** For roasted chicken, beef, hog, fish, lamb, and vegetables, AIR ROAST is the best solution. This option can be used to prepare major courses. A full-sized meals dish will have a crispy exterior and a perfectly cooked within. Meals are cooked in a fraction of the time it takes in an air fryer.

**REHEAT FUNCTION:** There's no need to be concerned about leftover foods or meals. There's also a REHEAT option on the Ninja Foodi Dual Heat Air Fry Oven. Insert the SearPlate or Wire Rack into the device with the food inside. Your meals will have a crunchy feel to them. The meals didn't need to be reheated on the stovetop.

**BROIL FUNCTION:** For broiling fish, meat, and vegetables, utilise the BROIL cooking function. It has the ability to brown casseroles and nachos. Insert the SearPlate or Wire Rack into the unit with the meat or fish on it.

**RAPID BAKE FUNCTION:** For frozen foods and baked dinners, RAPID BAKE is ideal. This cooking operation helps the dough rise even further and adds texture to the outside. This function can be used to make cookies, cakes, and brownies. Place the SearPlate in the unit and bake your items quickly.

**FRESH PIZZA FUNCTION:** The Ninja Foodi Dual Heat Air Fry Oven has a special cooking feature called "FRESH PIZZA." You can produce a crispy and delicious topping for your homemade pizza. Place the pizza ingredients in the SearPlate and place it in the unit for a delectable and appetising fresh pizza.

**BAGEL FUNCTION:** Up to six bagels halves can be toasted. Bagels in a dark tint are included in this bundle. For bagels, you didn't need to buy a toaster. Up to 6 bagels can be toasted at the same time. Arrange the bagels on the Wire Rack.

**DEHYDRATE FUNCTION:** Jerky and dried fruits benefit from dehydration. It's used to manufacture jerky and dried fruit by removing moisture. Fill the air fry basket halfway with dried fruit and place it in the device. Dehydrate cooking is used to dehydrate vegetables, meats, and nutritious snacks, among other things.

**FROZEN PIZZA FUNCTION:** The Ninja Foodi Dual Heat Air Fry Oven has a special cooking option called "Frozen pizza." From thin crust to thick crust, frozen pizza can be cooked. Fill the SearPlate with frozen pizza and place it in the oven. You'll get a fluffy pizza with a brown top.

**GRIDDLE FUNCTION:** You didn't have to put sandwiches and pancakes on the cooktop any longer. This cooking device has a GRIDDLE that will light brown breakfast goods such as tortillas, quesadillas, sandwiches, burgers, and other similar items. The GRIDDLE is ideal for preparing breakfast dishes.

**SEAR CRISP FUNCTION:** is ideal for thick-cut pork tenderloin, vegetables, entire roasts, chicken, or turkey. It produces golden, crispy dinners. SEAR CRISP is ideal for crispy casseroles, beef roasts, pork tenderloin, lamb chops, chicken tenders, and vegetable dishes, among other things.

**AIR FRY FUNCTION:** This method is ideal for preparing French fries, chicken wings, chicken drumsticks, and chicken nuggets, among other things. This cooking feature creates dishes that are crispy, fresh, and delectable. Little to no oil is used in this cooking technique. As a result, it makes nutritious meals for you.

**BAKE FUNCTION:** Use the BAKE cooking mode to make cakes, cookies, cupcakes, muffins, and brownies, among other things. For this cooking method, a SearPlate or Wire Rack can be used. Baking did not necessitate the use of an oven. The Ninja Foodi Dual Heat Air Fry Oven also has a bake function. Brown tops will appear on cakes, cupcakes, cookies, and muffins.

**TOAST FUNCTION:** For toasting bread slices, TOAST is the ideal alternative. Up to nine slices of bread can be toasted. This device comes with a dark toast colour. To toast the bread slices, you didn't need to buy a toaster. You can toast up to nine slices at once. Arrange the toast on the Wire Rack.

## How to Keep It Clean & Well-Maintained

After each use, the unit must be completely cleaned to avoid damage. The appliance can be cleaned through the following steps:

- Before cleaning, disconnect the unit from the outlet.
- Carefully remove all accessories from the unit and set it aside to cool.
- Use soapy, warm water to clean the SearPlate, and a non-abrasive sponge to clean it.
- Place the SearPlate in warm, soapy water overnight to clean it thoroughly. Use a sponge to clean it.
- Clean the Air Fry Basket and Wire Rack in the dishwasher using hot, soapy water.
- Do not put the appliance in the dishwasher. It can be cleaned with a moist cloth.
- To clean the attachments, avoid using chemical cleaners or hard scrubbers.

## How to Use the Ninja Foodi Dual Heat Air Fry Oven

Procedures for Using the Appliance in Step-by-Step Order

- Connect the power cord to a power socket.
- To choose the preferred function, click the Mode button and turn the dial.
- To pick the preferred temperature, press the time/slice button and turn the dial.

- ❖ Select the desired temperature by pressing the temperature/shade button and turning the dial.
- ❖ To start preheating, turn the setting dial; once the machine beeps, the preheating is complete.
- ❖ Close the oven door after sliding the food into the desired place. The timer will begin to count down.
- ❖ The machine will beep when the cooking is finished, and the LCD will indicate END HOT which means the end of the cooking cycle.

# Chapter 1: Breakfast

## Savory Parsley Soufflé

Preparation Time: 10 minutes
Cooking Time: 8 minutes
Servings: 1-2

### Recipe Ingredients:
- 2 tablespoons of light cream
- 2 eggs
- 1 tablespoon fresh parsley, chopped
- 1 fresh red chili pepper, chopped
- Salt, as required

### Cooking Instruction:
1. At first, Grease 2 soufflé dishes. In a bowl, add all the ingredients and beat until well combined.

2. Next, divide the mixture into prepared soufflé dishes. Select Air Oven Mode button of Ninja Foodi Dual Heat Air Fry Oven and turn the dial to select "Air Fry" mode.

3. Then, select Time/Slices button and again turn the dial to set the cooking time to 8 minutes.

4. Now push Temp/Shade button and rotate the dial to set the temperature at 390°F. Press "Start/Stop" button to start.

5. When the time beeps to indicate that it is preheated, open the oven door and grease the Sear Plate.

6. Next, arrange the soufflé dishes onto the SearPlate and insert in the oven. Once cooking time is completed, open the oven door and serve hot.

# Puffed Egg Tarts

Preparation Time: 15 minutes
Cooking Time: 21 minutes
Servings: 3-4

## Recipe Ingredients:
- ½ (17.3-ounce package) frozen puff pastry, thawed
- ¾ cup of Cheddar cheese, shredded
- 4 large eggs
- 1 tablespoon of fresh parsley, minced

## Cooking Instruction:
1. At first, spread the pastry sheet on a floured surface and cut it into 4 squares of equal size.

2. Next, place the four squares in the SearPlate of Ninja Foodi Dual Heat Air Fry Oven.

3. Transfer the SearPlate to Ninja Foodi Dual Heat Air Fry Oven and close the door and select "Air Fry" mode by rotating the dial.

4. Select Temp/Shade button and change the value to 300°F. Press the Time/Slices button and change the value to 10 minutes, then press Start/Stop to begin cooking.

5. Then, press the center of each pastry square using the back of a metal spoon, and divide cheese into these indentations. Crack one egg into each pastry.

6. Return to the oven and close its oven door, rotate the dial to select the "Air Fry" mode.

7. Press the Time/Slices button and again use the dial to set the cooking time to 11 minutes.

8. Finally, Press the Temp/Shade button and rotate the dial to set the temperature at 350°F. Garnish the squares with parsley. Serve warm.

# Potato & Corned Beef Casserole

Preparation Time: 15 minutes
Cooking Time: 1 hour 20 minutes
Servings: 2-3

## Recipe Ingredients:
- 3 Yukon Gold potatoes
- 2 tablespoons of unsalted butter
- ½ of onion, chopped
- 2 garlic cloves, minced
- 2 tablespoons of vegetable oil
- ½ teaspoon of salt
- 12 ounces of corned beef
- 3 eggs

## Cooking Instruction:
1. Firstly, press Air Oven Mode button of Ninja Foodi Dual Heat Air Fry Oven and turn the dial to select "Bake" mode.

2. Select Time/Slices button and again turn the dial to set the cooking time to 30 minutes.

3. Next, push Temp/shade button and rotate the dial to set the temperature at 350°F. Press "Start/Stop" button to start.

4. Once the unit beeps to indicate that it is preheated, open the oven door and grease the air fry basket.

5. Then, place the potatoes into the prepared air fry basket and insert in the oven.

6. Once cooking time is completed, open the oven door and transfer the potatoes onto a tray. Now, set it aside to cool for about 15 minutes.

7. After cooling, cut the potatoes into ½-inch-thick slices and keep aside. In a skillet, melt the butter over medium heat and cook the onion and garlic for about 10 minutes.

8. Remove from the heat and place the onion mixture into a casserole dish, and add the potato slices, oil, salt, and corned beef and mix well.

9. Select Air Oven Mode button of Ninja Foodi Dual Heat Air Fry Oven and turn the dial to select "Bake" mode.

10. Press Time/Slices button and again turn the dial to set the cooking time to 40 minutes.

11. Next, push Temp/Shade button and rotate the dial to set the temperature at 350°F/. Press "Start/Stop" button to start.

12. Once is timer is up to show that it is preheated, open the oven door and arrange the casserole dish over the wire rack and insert in the oven.

13. After 30 minutes of cooking, remove the casscrole dish and crack 3 eggs on top.

14. When cooking time is completed, open the oven door and serve immediately.

# Broiled Bacon

Preparation Time: 10 minutes
Cooking Time: 10 minutes
Servings: 5-6

## Recipe Ingredients:
- 1 pound of bacon

## Cooking Instruction:
1. At first, evenly distribute the bacon in the air fry basket.

2. Then, turn on your Ninja Foodi Dual Heat Air Fry Oven, rotate the knob to select "Broil" and Select the unit for 5 minutes at LO.

3. With tongs, remove the bacon and place it on a paper towel-lined dish. Allow cooling before serving.

# Banana Bread

Preparation Time: 15 minutes
Cooking Time: 25 minutes
Servings: 5-6

## Recipe Ingredients:
- 4 medium bananas, peeled and sliced
- ¼ cup of plain Greek yogurt
- large eggs
- ½ ounce of vanilla extract
- 10 ounces of all-purpose flour
- ¾ cup of sugar
- 3 ounces of oat flour
- 1 teaspoon of baking powder
- 1 teaspoon of baking soda
- ¾ teaspoon of kosher salt
- ¾ teaspoon of ground cinnamon
- ½ teaspoon of ground cloves
- ¼ teaspoon of ground nutmeg
- ¾ cup of coconut oil
- 1 cup of toasted pecan

## Cooking Instruction:
1. Firstly, layer a 10.5-inch-by-5.5-inch loaf pan with a parchment sheet and keep it aside. Mash the banana in a bowl and add eggs.

2. Add the vanilla, and Greek yogurt, then mix thoroughly, and cover the banana yogurt mixture and leave it for 30 minutes.

3. Meanwhile, mix cinnamon, flour, sugar, baking powder, oat flour, salt, baking soda, coconut oil, cloves, and nutmeg in a mixer.

4. Slowly add banana mash mixture to the flour and continue mixing until it becomes smooth. Fold in nuts and mix gently until evenly incorporated.

5. Spread this banana-nut batter in the prepared loaf pan, and transfer the loaf pan on wire rack in Ninja Foodi Dual Heat Air Fry Oven and close the door.

6. Next, select "Bake" mode by rotating the dial. Press the Times/Slices button and change the value to 25 minutes.

7. Press the Temp/Shade button and change the value to 350°F. Press Start/Stop to begin cooking.

8. Once cooking is complete, slice and serve.

# Breakfast Potatoes

Preparation Time: 10 minutes
Cooking Time: 25 minutes
Servings: 6-7

## Recipe Ingredients:
- pounds red potatoes, diced
- ½ cup of sweet onion, diced
- 2 green bell peppers, sliced
- 2 red bell peppers, sliced
- ½ teaspoon of garlic powder
- ½ teaspoon of seasoned salt
- ½ teaspoon of fennel seed
- Cooking spray

## Cooking Instruction:
1. Begin by prepping the veggies and, if necessary, chopping them, then apply a light application of cooking oil spray to the air fry basket.

2. Next, fill the air fry basket with all of the vegetables, and top evenly with seasonings.

3. Apply a generous application of cooking oil spray, while you turn on your Ninja Foodi Dual Heat Air Fry Oven and rotate the knob to select "Air Fry".

4. Select the timer for 20 minutes and the temperature for 360°F. You can check on the basket after around 10-15 minutes to mix or toss it up.

5. Serve once cooking is over.

# Sausage Patties

Preparation Time: 5 minutes
Cooking Time: 6 minutes
Servings: 5-6

## Recipe Ingredients:
- 1 pound of pork sausage patties
- Fennel seeds

## Cooking Instruction:
1. Begin by preparing the sausage by slicing it into patties or using new patties, then flavor it with fennel seed or your favorite seasoning.

2. Then, arrange in air fry basket in a uniform layer, while you turn on your Ninja Foodi Dual Heat Air Fry Oven and rotate the knob to select "Broil".

3. Select the timer for 8 minutes and temperature to LO. Cook for another 4 minutes after carefully flipping the patties.

4. Serve and enjoy!

# French Toast

Preparation Time: 5 minutes
Cooking Time: 6 minutes
Servings: 3-4

## Recipe Ingredients:
- 1 cup of heavy cream
- 1 egg, beaten
- ¼ powdered sugar
- 1 teaspoon of cinnamon
- 8 slices of bread

## Cooking Instruction:
1. At first, place your bread on the wire rack. Turn on your Ninja Foodi Dual Heat Air Fry Oven.

2. Rotate the knob to select "Air Roast", then, select the timer for 4 minutes and the temperature for 390°F.

3. While the bread is toasting, combine the remaining ingredients in a mixing bowl.

4. Dip bread in batches into the mixture, making sure both sides are evenly covered. Place them on the air fry basket.

5. Next, turn on your Ninja Foodi Dual Heat Air Fry Oven and rotate the knob to select "Air Fry".

6. Select the timer for 4 minutes and the temperature for 390°F.

7. Serve with butter.

# Hard Boiled Eggs

**Preparation Time:** 5 minutes
**Cooking Time:** 12 minutes
**Servings:** 5-6

**Recipe Ingredients:**
- 6 eggs

**Cooking Instruction:**
1. Add the eggs in the air fry basket, and turn on your Ninja Foodi Dual Heat Air Fry Oven and rotate the knob to select "Air Fry".

2. Select the timer for 12 minutes and the temperature for 300°F and allow to cook.

3. After the cooking time has been elapsed, immerse for 5 minutes in a bowl of icy water. After that, peel and serve.

# Breakfast Pizzas with Muffins

Preparation Time: 5 minutes
Cooking Time: 6 minutes
Servings: 2-3

## Recipe Ingredients:
- 6 eggs, cooked and scrambled
- 1 pound of ground sausage
- ½ cup of Colby jack cheese, shredded
- 3 egg muffins, sliced in half
- Olive oil spray

## Cooking Instruction:
1. Start by using an olive oil cooking spray to spray the air fry basket, then place each half in the basket.

2. Next, using a light layer of olive oil spray, lightly coat the English muffins and top with scrambled eggs and fried sausages. Add cheese on top of each one.

3. Turn on your Ninja Foodi Dual Heat Air Fry Oven and rotate the knob to select "Bake".

4. Select the timer for 5 minutes and the temperature for 355°F.

5. Serve hot.

# Breakfast Casserole

Preparation Time: 15 minutes
Cooking Time: 30 minutes
Servings: 7-8

## Recipe Ingredients:
- 8 eggs
  - 1 pound of pork sausage
  - 1½ cups of whole milk
  - 850g frozen hash browns, shredded
  - 2 cups of cheddar cheese
  - 1½ teaspoons of salt
  - ¼ teaspoon of garlic powder

## Cooking Instruction:

1. Begin by tossing the uncooked ground sausage into the pan. Sauté and cook for 6-8 minutes, or until sausage is browned.

2. Once done, mix in the frozen hash browns thoroughly, also Mix in 1 cup of cheese. Whisk together the eggs, Cheddar cheese, and spices in a separate basin.

3. Fill the pot with the egg mixture. Place the mixture into the SearPlate.

4. Turn on your Ninja Foodi Dual Heat Air Fry Oven and rotate the knob to select "Air Fry."

5. Select the timer for 30 minutes and the temperature for 350°F.

6. Serve while hot.

# Hash Browns

Preparation Time: 5 minutes
Cooking Time: 5 minutes
Servings: 1-2

## Recipe Ingredients:
- 4 hash brown patties
- Cooking oil spray

## Cooking Instruction:
1. At first, coat the air fry basket with your preferred cooking oil spray, then place the hash brown patties in the oven in an even layer.

2. Spray them with your favorite cooking oil spray, then turn on your Ninja Foodi Dual Heat Air Fry Oven and rotate the knob to select "Air Fry".

3. Select the timer for 5 minutes and the temperature for 390°F . once done dish out and serve immediately.

# Date Bread

**Preparation Time:** 15 minutes
**Cooking Time:** 22 minutes
**Servings:** 9-10

## Recipe Ingredients:
- 2½ cups of dates, pitted and chopped
- ¼ cup of butter
- 1 cup of hot water
- 1½ cups of flour
- ½ cup of brown sugar
- 1 teaspoon of baking powder
- 1 teaspoon of baking soda
- ½ teaspoon of salt
- 1 egg

## Cooking Instruction:
1. In a large bowl, add the dates and butter and top with the hot water. Set aside for about 5 minutes.

2. In another bowl, mix the flour, brown sugar, baking powder, baking soda, and salt together.

3. Meanwhile In the bowl of dates, add the flour mixture and the egg and mix well. Grease SearPlate, place the mixture into the prepared SearPlate.

4. Press Air Oven Mode button of Ninja Foodi Dual Heat Air Fry Oven and turn the dial to select "Air Fry" mode.

5. Press Time/Slices button and again turn the dial to set the cooking time to 22 minutes. Now push Temp/Shade button.

6. Rotate the dial to set the temperature at 340°F, press "Start/Stop" button to start. When the unit beeps to indicate that it is preheated, open the oven door. Insert the SearPlate in the oven.

7. Once the cooking time is completed, open the oven door and place the SearPlate onto a wire rack for about 10-15 minutes.

8. Carefully, invert the bread onto the wire rack to cool completely cool before slicing. Cut the bread into desired sized slices and serve.

# Savory Sausage & Beans Muffins

Preparation Time: 15 minutes
Cooking Time: 20 minutes
Servings: 5-6

## Recipe Ingredients:
- 4 eggs
- ½ cup of cheddar cheese, shredded
- 3 tablespoons of heavy cream
- 1 tablespoon of tomato paste
- ¼ teaspoon of salt
- Pinch of freshly ground black pepper
- Cooking spray
- 4 cooked breakfast sausage links, chopped
- 3 tablespoons of baked beans

## Cooking Instruction:
1. Start by greasing a 6-cup muffin pan. In a bowl, add the eggs, cheddar cheese, heavy cream, tomato paste, salt and black pepper and beat until well combined.

2. Stir in the sausage pieces and beans, and divide the mixture into prepared muffin cups evenly.

3. Press Air Oven Mode button of Ninja Foodi Dual Heat Air Fry Oven and turn the dial to select "Bake" mode.

4. Press Time/Slices button and again turn the dial to set the cooking time to 20 minutes. Now push Temp/Shade button.

5. Rotate the dial to set the temperature at 350°F. Press "Start/Stop" button to start.

6. When the unit beeps to show that it is preheated, open the oven door. Arrange the muffin pan over the wire rack and insert in the oven.

7. When cooking time is completed, open the oven door and place the muffin pan onto a wire rack to cool for 5 minutes before serving.

# Blueberry-Lemon Scones

Preparation Time: 15 minutes
Cooking Time: 25 minutes
Servings: 5-6

## Recipe Ingredients:
- **2 cups of all-purpose flour**
- 1 tablespoon of baking powder
- 2 teaspoons of sugar
- 1 teaspoon of kosher salt
- 2 ounces of refined coconut oil
- 1 cup of fresh blueberries
- ¼ ounce of lemon zest
- 8 ounces of coconut milk

## Cooking Instruction:

1. Firstly, blend coconut oil with salt, sugar, baking powder, and flour in a food processor. Transfer this flour mixture to a mixing bowl.

2. Now add coconut milk and lemon zest to the flour mixture, then mix well. Fold in blueberries and mix the prepared dough well until smooth.

3. Spread this blueberry dough into a 7-inch round and place it in a pan. Then, refrigerate the blueberry dough for 15 minutes, slice it into 6 wedges.

4. Layer the SearPlate with a parchment sheet. Place the blueberry wedges in the lined SearPlate.

5. Transfer the scones to Ninja Foodi Dual Heat Air Fry Oven and close the door. Select "Bake" mode by rotating the dial.

6. Then, press the Times/Slices button and change the value to 25 minutes. Press the Temp/Shade button and change the value to 400°F.

7. Press Start/Stop to begin cooking.

8. Serve fresh.

# Mushrooms Frittata

Preparation Time: 15 minutes
Cooking Time: 15 minutes
Servings: 1-2

## Recipe Ingredients:
- **1 cup of egg whites**
- 2 tablespoons of skim milk
- ¼ cup of tomato, sliced
- ¼ cup of mushrooms, sliced
- 2 tablespoons of fresh chives, chopped
- Black pepper, to taste

## Cooking Instruction:
1. At first, beat egg whites with mushrooms and the rest of the ingredients in a bowl.

2. Spread this egg white mixture in SearPlate, then transfer the dish to Ninja Foodi Dual Heat Air Fry Oven and close the door.

3. Select "Air Fry" mode by rotating the dial. Press the Time/Slices button and change the value to 15 minutes.

4. Press the Temp/Shade button and change the value to 320°F. Press Start/Stop to begin cooking.

5. When it beeps to signify it has preheated, insert the SearPlate into the oven. Close the oven door and let it cook.

6. Slice and serve warm.

# Ham and Cheese Scones

**Preparation Time:** 15 minutes
**Cooking Time:** 25 minutes
**Servings:** 5-6

## Recipe Ingredients:
- 2 cups of all-purpose flour
- 1 tablespoon of baking powder
- 2 teaspoons of sugar
- 1 teaspoon of kosher salt
- 2 tablespoons of butter, cubed
- 1 cup of ham, diced, cooked
- ¼ cup of scallion, chopped
- 4 ounces of cheddar cheese, shredded
- ¼ cup of milk
- ¾ cup of heavy cream

## Cooking Instruction:

1. At first, whisk baking powder with flour, sugar, salt, and butter in a mixing bowl. Beat milk, cream, ham, scallion, and cheddar cheese in another bowl.

2. Then, stir in the flour-butter mixture and mix well until it forms a smooth dough. Place this scones dough on a floured surface.

3. Spread it into a 7-inch round sheet. Cut this dough sheet into 6 wedges of equal size. Place these wedges in the SearPlate, lined with parchment paper.

4. Transfer the SearPlate to Ninja Foodi Dual Heat Air Fry Oven and close the door. Select "Bake" mode by rotating the dial.

5. Press the Time/Slices button and change the value to 25 minutes. Press the Temp/Shade button and change the value to 400°F.

6. Press Start/Stop to begin cooking. When baked, serve the scones with morning eggs.

# Sweet & Spiced Toasts

Preparation Time: 10 minutes
Cooking Time: 4 minutes
Servings: 2-3

## Recipe Ingredients:
- ¼ cup of sugar
- ½ teaspoon of ground cinnamon
- ⅛ teaspoon of ground cloves
- ⅛ teaspoon of ground ginger
- ½ teaspoons of vanilla extract
- ¼ cup of salted butter, softened
- 6 bread slices
- Pepper, as you need

## Cooking Instruction:
1. In a bowl, add the sugar, vanilla, cinnamon, pepper, and butter. Mix until smooth.

2. Then, spread the butter mixture evenly over each bread slice, and press Air Oven Mode button of Ninja Foodi Dual Heat Air Fry Oven.

3. Turn the dial to select "Air Fry" mode. Next, press Times/Slices button and again turn the dial to set the cooking time to 4 minutes.

4. Now push Temp/Shade button and rotate the dial to set the temperature at 400°F. Press "Start/Stop" button to start.

5. When the unit beeps to show that it is preheated, open the oven door and grease the air fry basket.

6. Place the bread slices into the prepared air fry basket, buttered-side up. and insert in the oven.

7. Flip the slices once halfway through. When cooking time is completed, open the oven door and transfer the French toasts onto a platter.

8. Serve warm.

# Raisin Bran Muffins

**Preparation Time:** 15 minutes
**Cooking Time:** 18 minutes
**Servings:** 5-6

## Recipe Ingredients:
- 1 cup of wheat bran
- 1 cup of boiling water
- 4 ounces of plain, non-fat Greek yogurt
- 2 large eggs
- 1½ cups of whole wheat flour
- 5½ ounces of all-purpose flour
- ¾ cup of sugar
- ½ ounce of ground cinnamon
- 2 teaspoons of baking powder
- ¾ teaspoon of kosher salt or sea salt
- ¼ teaspoon of baking soda
- ⅛ teaspoon of grated nutmeg
- 6 ounces of butter
- 1 cup of golden raisins
- ¾ ounce of flaxseed

## Cooking Instruction:

1. Firstly, mix wheat bran with boiling water in a bowl and leave it for 5 minutes.

2. Add eggs, wheat flour, sugar, Greek yogurt, cinnamon, salt, baking soda, baking powder, butter, and nutmeg into the wheat bran, then mix well in a mixer.

3. Stir in raisins and mix the batter gently. Divide this bran muffin batter into 12 greased muffin cups.

4. Transfer the muffin cups on wire rack in Ninja Foodi Dual Heat Air Fry Oven and close the door.

5. Select "Bake" mode by rotating the dial. Press the Time/Slices button and change the value to 18 minutes.

6. Select the Temp/Shade button and change the value to 400°F. Press Start/Stop to begin cooking.

7. Serve fresh.

# Egg in Hole

**Preparation Time:** 5 minutes
Cooking Time: 10 minutes
Servings: 1-2

## Recipe Ingredients:
- 1 piece toast
- 1 egg
- Salt and pepper, to taste

## Cooking Instruction:
1. Start by using a nonstick cooking spray to spray SearPlate, then place a piece of bread on the SearPlate.

2. Remove the bread by poking a hole in it with a cup or a cookie cutter. into the hole, crack the egg.

3. Turn on your Ninja Foodi Dual Heat Air Fry Oven and rotate the knob to select "Air Fry".

4. Select the timer for 6 minutes and the temperature for 330°F. When it beeps to signify it has preheated, insert the SearPlate in the oven.

5. Dish out and sprinkle with salt and pepper to serve.

# Breakfast Bake

Preparation Time: 15 minutes
Cooking Time: 50 minutes
Servings: 5-6

## Recipe Ingredients:
- 24 ounces of bulk pork sausage
- 1 medium bell pepper, chopped
- 1 medium onion, chopped
- 3 cups of frozen hash brown potatoes
- 2 cups of shredded Cheddar cheese
- 1 cup of Bisquick mix
- 2 cups of milk
- ¼ teaspoon of pepper
- 4 eggs

## Cooking Instruction:
1. At first, whisk Bisquick with milk, eggs, and pepper in a mixer. Sauté pork sausage, onion, and bell pepper in a 10-inch skillet over medium heat.

2. Stir cook until the sausage turns brown in color, then transfer to SearPlate. Next, toss in potatoes, 1½ cups of cheese, and the Bisquick mixture.

3. Then, transfer the SearPlate to Ninja Foodi Dual Heat Air Fry Oven and close the door. Select "Bake" mode by rotating the dial.

4. Press the TIME/SLICES button and change the value to 45 minutes. Press the TEMP/SHADE button and change the value to 350°F.

5. Press Start/Stop to begin cooking. Drizzle the remaining cheese over the casserole and bake for 5 minutes.

6. Serve and enjoy!

# Chapter 2: Snacks & Appetizer Recipes

## Roasted Cashews

Preparation Time: 5 minutes
Cooking Time: 5 minutes
Servings: 5-6

### Recipe Ingredients:
- 1½ cups of raw cashew nuts
- 1 teaspoon of butter, melted
- Salt and freshly ground black pepper, as required

### Cooking Instructions:
1. Start by mixing all the ingredients together in a bowl. Press AIR OVEN MODE button of Ninja Foodi Dual Heat Air Fry Oven.

2. Turn the dial to select "Air Fry" mode. Press Time/Slices button and again turn the dial to set the cooking time to 5 minutes.

3. Then, push Temp/Shade button and rotate the dial to set the temperature at 355°F. Press "Start/Stop" button to start.

4. Once the timer is up to signify it is preheated, carefully open the oven door. Arrange the cashews into the air fry basket and insert in the oven.

5. Shake the cashews once halfway through. Once cooking is completed, open the oven door and transfer the cashews into a heatproof bowl.

6. Serve warm.

# Pasta Chips

Preparation Time: 15 minutes
Cooking Time: 10 minutes
Servings: 3-4

## Recipe Ingredients:
- ½ tablespoon of olive oil
- ½ tablespoon of nutritional yeast
- 1 cup of bow tie pasta
- ⅔ teaspoon of Italian Seasoning Blend
- ¼ teaspoon of salt

## Cooking Instruction:
1. Cook and boil the pasta in salted water in half of the time as stated on the box, then drain it.

2. Then, toss the boiled pasta with salt, Italian seasoning, nutritional yeast, and olive oil in a bowl. Spread this pasta in the air fry basket.

3. Next, transfer the basket to Ninja Foodi Dual Heat Air Fry Oven and close the door. Select "Air Fry" mode by rotating the dial.

4. Select the Time/Slices button and change the value to 5 minutes. Press the TEMP/SHADE button and change the value to 390°F.

5. Press Start/Stop to begin cooking. Finally, toss the pasta and continue air frying for another 5 minutes.

6. Serve and enjoy!

# Fiesta Chicken Fingers

Preparation Time: **15** minutes
Cooking Time: 12 minutes
Servings: 3-4

## Recipe Ingredients:
- ¾ pound boneless chicken breasts, cut into strips
- ½ cup buttermilk
- ¼ teaspoon pepper
- 1 cup all-purpose flour
- Cups of corn chips, crushed
- 1 envelope taco seasoning

## For Serving:
- Sour cream ranch dip or Fresh salsa

## Cooking Instruction:
1. Coat the chicken with pepper and flour, then mix corn chips with taco seasoning. Dip the chicken fingers in the buttermilk evenly.

2. Then, coat with the corn chips. Once done, place the chicken fingers in the air fry basket and spray with cooking oil.

3. Transfer the basket to Ninja Foodi Dual Heat Air Fry Oven and close the door. Select "Air Fry" mode by rotating the dial.

4. Press the Time/Slices button and change the value to 12 minutes. Press the TEMP/SHADE button and change the value to 325°F.

5. Press Start/Stop to begin cooking. Flip the Chicken fingers once cooked halfway through, then resume cooking.

6. Serve warm with sour cream ranch dip or fresh salsa.

# Bacon-Wrapped Filled Jalapeno

Preparation Time: 10 minutes
Cooking Time: 15 minutes
Servings: 5-6

## Recipe Ingredients:
- 12 jalapenos
- 226g cream cheese
- ½ cup of cheddar cheese, shredded
- ¼ teaspoon of garlic powder
- 1/8 teaspoon of onion powder
- 12 slices of bacon, thinly cut
- Salt and pepper, to taste

## Cooking Instruction:
1. Discard the seeds from the jalapenos by cutting them in half and removing the stems.

2. Next, combine cream cheese, shredded cheddar cheese, garlic powder, onion powder, salt, and pepper. To blend, stir everything together.

3. Fill each jalapeno just to the top with the cream mixture using a tiny spoon. Now, turn on Ninja Foodi Dual Heat Air Fry Oven and rotate the knob to select "Bake".

4. Preheat by selecting the timer for 15 minute and temperature for 350°F. Press START/STOP to begin. Cut each slice of bacon in half.

5. Wrap one piece of bacon around each half of a jalapeño. Meanwhile, in the SearPlate, arrange the bacon-wrapped filled jalapenos in an even layer.

6. When the unit beeps to signify it has preheated, insert the SearPlate in the oven. Close the oven and let it cook.

7. Serve and enjoy!

# Baked Mozzarella Sticks

**Preparation Time:** 5 minutes
Cooking Time: 8 minutes
Servings: 5-6

**Recipe Ingredients:**
- ½ cup of Italian Style breadcrumbs
- ¾ cup of panko break crumbs
- ¼ cup of parmesan cheese
- 1 tablespoon of garlic powder
- 12 mozzarella cheese sticks
- Cooking spray

## Cooking Instruction:

1. Make mozzarella sticks by freezing them for an hour or two. Take the mozzarella sticks out of the fridge and cut them in half so that each one is 2-3 inches long.

2. Then, combine the Panko, Italian Style bread crumbs, parmesan cheese, and garlic powder on a dish and stir well.

3. Whisk together the eggs in a separate bowl, then cover the mozzarella stick completely with egg with a fork and dip and totally cover the mozzarella stick in the breadcrumb mixture.

4. Meanwhile, on a nonstick pan, carefully arrange mozzarella sticks in a single layer. Freeze for an hour and take the mozzarella sticks out of the freezer.

5. Dip them in the egg and breadcrumb mixture once more. Using cooking spray, lightly coat the SearPlate. Place the cheese sticks.

6. Turn on Ninja Foodi Dual Heat Air Fry Oven and rotate the knob to select "Bake". Select the timer for 10 minutes and the temperature for 360°F.

7. Remove and serve.

# Corn on the Cob

Preparation Time: 5 minutes
Cooking Time: 13 minutes
Servings: 1-2

## Recipe Ingredients:
- 2 ears corn
- 2 tablespoons of butter, melted
- ½ teaspoon of dried parsley
- ¼ teaspoon of sea salt
- 2 tablespoons of parmesan cheese, shredded

## Cooking Instruction:
1. Firstly, remove any silk from both ears of corn. If desired, cut corns in half.

2. In a mixing dish, combine melted butter, parsley, and sea salt. Using a pastry brush, evenly coat the corn. If used, wrap corn with foil.

3. Place corn inside the SearPlate side by side. Place it inside the oven. Turn on Ninja Foodi Dual Heat Air Fry Oven and rotate the knob to select "Air Roast".

4. Select the timer for 12 minutes and the temperature for 350°F. Remove from Ninja Foodi Dual Heat Air Fry Oven to serve hot.

# Air Fryer Ravioli

**Preparation Time:** 5 minutes
Cooking Time: 10 minutes
Servings: 1-2

## Recipe Ingredients:
- 12 frozen ravioli
- ½ cup of buttermilk
- ½ cup of Italian breadcrumbs
- Cooking oil

## Cooking Instruction:
1. Place two bowls next to each other. In one, put the buttermilk, and in the other, put the breadcrumbs.

2. Dip Each ravioli piece in buttermilk and then breadcrumbs, making sure it is well coated.

3. Place each breaded ravioli in a single layer in the air fry basket and spritz the tops halfway through with oil.

4. Place it inside the oven. Turn on Ninja Foodi Dual Heat Air Fry Oven and rotate the knob to select "Air Fry".

5. Select the timer for 7 minutes and the temperature for 400°F. Remove from Ninja Foodi Dual Heat Air Fry Oven to serve hot.

# *Zucchini Chips*

**Preparation Time:** 10 minutes
**Cooking Time:** 13 minutes
**Servings:** 5-6

## Recipe Ingredients:
- 2 large zucchinis, sliced
- ¾ cup of panko bread crumbs
- 1 teaspoon of Old bay
- 1 teaspoon of garlic salt
- 1 egg, beaten
- Olive oil spray

## Cooking Instruction:
1. Combine the Panko and seasoning on a dish and stir well. In a separate bowl, whisk the egg.

2. Dip zucchini slices in the egg one at a time, then coat with the bread crumb mixture on all sides.

3. Using olive oil cooking spray, lightly coat the air fry basket. Place the zucchini in the air fry basket gently.

4. Turn on Ninja Foodi Dual Heat Air Fry Oven and rotate the knob to select "Air Fry". Select the timer for 13 minutes and the temperature for 350°F.

5. Remove and enjoy immediately.

# Sweet Potato Fries

Preparation Time: 10 minutes
Cooking Time: 15 minutes
Servings: 3-4

## Recipe Ingredients:
- 3 sweet potatoes, cut into fries
- 2 tablespoons of olive oil
- ½ teaspoon of salt
- ¼ teaspoon of black pepper
- ½ teaspoon of garlic powder

## Cooking Instruction:
1. Slice sweet potatoes into ½-¼ inch-thick French fry slices. Using olive oil cooking spray, lightly coat the air fry basket.

2. Next, pour the olive oil, salt, pepper, paprika, and garlic powder over the sweet potatoes in a mixing bowl. To coat them, combine them thoroughly.

3. Place each sweet potato fry in the basket in a uniform layer. Place inside the oven. Turn on Ninja Foodi Dual Heat Air Fry Oven.

4. Rotate the knob to select "Broil". Select the unit for 12 minutes at LOW. Serve immediately after cooking.

# French Toast Bites

**Preparation Time:** 5 minutes
**Cooking Time:** 10 minutes
**Servings:** 1-2

## Recipe Ingredients:
- ½ loaf of brioche bread
- 3 eggs
- 1 tablespoon of milk
- 1 teaspoon of vanilla
- ½ teaspoon of cinnamon

## Cooking Instruction:
1. In a large mixing bowl, cut half a loaf of bread into cubes, combine the eggs, milk, vanilla, and cinnamon in a small mixing dish.

2. Pour the mixture over the slices and toss to coat. In greased air fry basket, arrange bread slices in a single layer. Place inside the oven.

3. Turn on Ninja Foodi Dual Heat Air Fry Oven and rotate the knob to select "Air Fry". Select the timer for 10 minutes and the temperature for 390°F.

4. Remove from Ninja Foodi Dual Heat Air Fry Oven to serve.

# Cauliflower Poppers

Preparation Time: 10 minutes
Cooking Time: 20 minutes
Servings: 5-6

## Recipe Ingredients:
- 3 tablespoons olive oil
- 1 teaspoon of paprika
- ½ teaspoon of ground cumin
- ¼ teaspoon of ground turmeric
- Salt and ground black pepper, as required
- 1 medium head cauliflower, cut into florets

## Cooking Instruction:
1. In a bowl, place all ingredients and toss to coat well. Place the cauliflower mixture in the greased SearPlate.

2. Press Air Oven Mode button of Ninja Foodi Dual Heat Air Fry Oven and turn the dial to select the "Bake" mode.

3. Press Time/Slices button and again turn the dial to set the cooking time to 20 minutes. Now, push Temp/Shade button.

4. Rotate the dial to set the temperature at 450°F. Press "Start/Stop" button to start. When the unit beeps to show that it is preheated.

5. Open the oven door and insert the SearPlate in oven. Flip the cauliflower mixture once halfway through.

6. When cooking time is completed, open the oven door and transfer the cauliflower poppers onto a platter. Serve warm.

# Persimmon Chips

Preparation Time: 10 minutes
Cooking Time: 10 minutes
Servings: 1-2

## Recipe Ingredients:
- 2 ripe persimmons, cut into slices horizontally
- Salt and ground black pepper, as required

## Cooking Instruction:
1. Arrange the persimmons slices onto the greased SearPlate. Press Air Oven Mode button of Ninja Foodi Dual Heat Air Fry Oven.

2. Turn the dial to select "Air Fry" mode. Next, press Time/Slices button and again turn the dial to set the cooking time to 10 minutes.

3. Now push Temp/Shade button and rotate the dial to set the temperature at 400°F. Press "Start/Stop" button to start.

4. When the unit beeps to show that it is preheated, open the oven door. Next, Insert the SearPlate in oven, and flip the chips once halfway through.

5. Once cooking time is completed, open the oven door and transfer the chips onto a platter. Serve warm.

# Carrot Chips

Preparation Time: 15 minutes
Cooking Time: 15 minutes
Servings: 7-8

## Recipe Ingredients:
- 2 pounds of carrots, sliced
- ¼ cup of olive oil
- 1 tablespoon of sea salt
- 1 teaspoon of ground cumin
- 1 teaspoon of ground cinnamon

## Cooking Instruction:
1. Toss the carrot slices with oil, sea salt, cumin, and cinnamon in a large bowl.

2. Next, grease the SearPlate and spread the carrot slices in it. Transfer the SearPlate to Ninja Foodi Dual Heat Air Fry Oven and close the door.

3. Select "Bake" mode by rotating the dial. Press the TIME/SLICES button and change the value to 15 minutes.

4. Press the TEMP/SHADE button and change the value to 450°F. Press Start/Stop to begin cooking.

5. Flip the chips after 7-8 minutes of cooking and resume baking.

6. Serve fresh.

# Tofu Nuggets

Preparation Time: 10 minutes
Cooking Time: 15 minutes
Servings: 3-4

## Recipe Ingredients:
- 400g extra firm tofu
- 1/3 cup of nutritional yeast
- ¼ cup of water
- 1 tablespoon of garlic powder
- 1 teaspoon of onion powder
- 1 teaspoon of sweet paprika
- 1 teaspoon of poultry spice

## Cooking Instruction:
1. Press the tofu for 10 minutes. Add all ingredients to a bowl and stir to combine.

2. Over the bowl, break the tofu into bite-sized chunks. Use your thumb to create rough, rounded edges as you go.

3. Carefully fold the chunks into the paste gently, taking care not to break the tofu, and place the tofu in air fry basket in a single layer.

4. Turn on Ninja Foodi Dual Heat Air Fry Oven and rotate the knob to select "Air Fry". Select the timer for 15 minutes and the temperature for 350°F.

5. Halfway through, pause and shake the basket.

6. Serve immediately or save for later.

# Chicken & Parmesan Nuggets

Preparation Time: 15 minutes
Cooking Time: 10 minutes
Servings: 5-6

## Recipe Ingredients:
- 2 large chicken breasts, cut into 1-inch cubes
- 1 cup of breadcrumbs
- ⅓ tablespoon of Parmesan cheese, shredded
- 1 teaspoon of onion powder
- ¼ teaspoon of smoked paprika
- Salt and ground black pepper, as required

## Cooking Instruction:
1. In a large resealable bag, add all the ingredients, then seal the bag and shake well to coat completely.

2. Press AIR OVEN MODE button of Ninja Foodi Dual Heat Air Fry Oven and turn the dial to select "Air Fry" mode.

3. Press TIME/SLICES button and again turn the dial to set the cooking time to 10 minutes.

4. Now push TEMP/SHADE button and rotate the dial to set the temperature at 400°F. Press "Start/Stop" button to start.

5. Once the unit beeps to show that it is preheated, open the oven door. Arrange the nuggets into the air fry basket and insert in the oven.

6. When cooking time is completed, open the oven door and transfer the nuggets onto a platter.

# Onion Rings

Preparation Time: 15 minutes
Cooking Time: 15 minutes
Servings: 3-4

## Recipe Ingredients:
- ½ cup of all-purpose flour
- 1 teaspoon of paprika
- 1 teaspoon of salt, divided
- ½ cup of buttermilk
- 1 egg
- 1 cup of panko breadcrumbs
- 2 tablespoons of olive oil
- 1 large yellow sweet onion, sliced ½-inch-thick rings

## Cooking Instruction:

1. Mix flour with paprika and salt on a plate. Coat the onion rings with the flour mixture. In a bowl, beat egg with buttermilk.

2. Dip all the onion rings with the egg mixture inside. Spread the breadcrumbs in a bowl. Now, coat the onion rings with breadcrumbs.

3. Place the onion rings in the air fry basket and spray them with cooking oil. Transfer the basket to Ninja Foodi Dual Heat Air Fry Oven and close the door.

4. Select "Air Fry" mode by rotating the dial. Press the TEMP/SHADE button and change the value to 400°F.

5. Press the TIME/SLICES button and change the value to 15 minutes, then press Start/Stop to begin cooking.

6. Serve warm.

# Baked Potatoes

Preparation Time: 15 minutes
Cooking Time: 45 minutes
Servings: 3-4

## Recipe Ingredients:
- 3 russet potatoes, scrubbed and rinsed
- Cooking spray
- ½ teaspoon of sea salt
- ½ teaspoon of garlic powder

## Cooking Instruction:
1. Rub the potatoes with salt and garlic powder. Place the potatoes in the air fry basket and spray with cooking spray.

2. Transfer the basket to Ninja Foodi Dual Heat Air Fry Oven and close the door.

3. Select the "Bake" mode by rotating the dial. Press the TIME/SLICES button and change the value to 45 minutes.

4. Press the TEMP/SHADE button and change the value to 350°F. Press Start/Stop to begin cooking.

5. Make a slit on top of potatoes and score the flesh inside.

# Eggplant Fries

Preparation Time: 15 minutes
Cooking Time: 10 minutes
Servings: 3-4

## Recipe Ingredients:
- 2 large eggs
- ½ cup of grated Parmesan cheese
- ½ cup of toasted wheat germ
- 1 teaspoon of Italian seasoning
- ¾ teaspoon of garlic salt
- 1 (1¼-pound) eggplant, peeled
- Cooking spray
- 1 cup of meatless pasta sauce, warmed

## Cooking Instruction:
1. Cut the eggplant into sticks. Mix parmesan cheese, wheat germ, seasoning, and garlic salt in a bowl.

2. Coat the eggplant sticks with the parmesan mixture. Place the eggplant fries in the air fry basket and spray them with cooking spray.

3. Transfer the basket to Ninja Foodi Dual Heat Air Fry Oven and close the door. Select "Air Fry" mode by rotating the dial.

4. Press the TIME/SLICES button and change the value to 10 minutes. Next, press the Temp/Shade button and change the value to 375°F.

5. Press Start/Stop to begin cooking. Serve warm with marinara sauce.

# Potato Chips

Preparation Time: 15 minutes
Cooking Time: 25 minutes
Servings: 1-2

## Recipe Ingredients:
- 1 medium Russet potato, sliced
- 1 tablespoon of canola oil
- ¼ teaspoon of sea salt
- ¼ teaspoon of black pepper
- 1 teaspoon of chopped fresh rosemary

## Cooking Instruction:
1. At first, fill a suitable glass bowl with cold water and add sliced potatoes. Leave the potatoes for 20 minutes, then drain them.

2. Pat dry the chips with a paper towel. Toss the potatoes with salt, black pepper, and oil to coat well. Then, spread the potato slices in the air fry basket evenly.

3. Transfer the basket to Ninja Foodi Dual Heat Air Fry Oven and close the door. Select "Air Fry" mode by rotating the dial.

4. Press the TIME/SLICES button and change the value to 25 minutes. Press the TEMP/SHADE button and change the value to 375°F.

5. Press Start/Stop to begin cooking. Garnish with rosemary. Serve warm.

# Avocado Fries

Preparation Time: 15 minutes
Cooking Time: 20 minutes
Servings: 3-4

## Recipe Ingredients:
- ½ cup of panko breadcrumbs
- ½ teaspoon of salt
- 1 avocado, peeled, pitted, and sliced
- 1 cup of egg, whisked

## Cooking Instruction:
1. Toss breadcrumbs with salt in a shallow bowl. Then, dip the avocado strips in the egg, then coat them with panko.

2. Spread these slices in the air fry basket. Transfer the sandwich to Ninja Foodi Dual Heat Air Fry Oven and close the door.

3. Select "Bake" mode by rotating the dial. Press the Time/Slices button and change the value to 20 minutes.

4. Press the Temp/Shade button and change the value to 400°F. Press Start/Stop to begin cooking. Serve fresh.

# Chapter 3: Vegetables & Slides Recipes

## Wine Braised Mushrooms

**Preparation Time:** 10 minutes
Cooking Time: 32 minutes
Servings: 5-6

### Recipe Ingredients:
- 1 tablespoon of butter
- 2 teaspoons of Herbs de Provence
- ½ teaspoon of garlic powder
- 2 pounds of fresh mushrooms, quartered
- 2 tablespoons of white wine

### Cooking Instruction:
1. In a frying pan, mix together the butter, Herbs de Provence, and garlic powder over medium-low heat and stir fry for about 2 minutes.

2. Stir in the mushrooms and remove from the heat. Transfer the mushroom mixture into a SearPlate.

3. Select Air Oven Mode button of Ninja Foodi Dual Heat Air Fry Oven and turn the dial to select "Air Fry" mode.

4. Press TIME/SLICES button and again turn the dial to set the cooking time to 30 minutes.

5. Now push TEMP/SHADE button and rotate the dial to set the temperature at 320°F. Press "Start/Stop" button to start.

6. When the unit beeps to indicate that it is preheated, open the oven door. Insert the SearPlate in the oven.

7. After 25 minutes of cooking, stir the wine into mushroom mixture, and when cooking time is completed, open the oven door and serve hot.

# Broccoli Casserole

Preparation Time: 15 minutes
Cooking Time: 45 minutes
Servings: 5-6

## Recipe Ingredients:
- 1 cup of mayonnaise
- 10½ ounces of cream of celery soup
- 2 large eggs, beaten
- 20 ounces of chopped broccoli
- 2 tablespoons of onion, minced
- 1 cup of Cheddar cheese, grated
- 1 tablespoon of Worcestershire sauce
- 1 teaspoon of seasoned salt
- Black pepper, to taste
- 2 tablespoons of butter

## Cooking Instruction:

1. Whisk mayonnaise with eggs, condensed soup in a large bowl. Stir in salt, black pepper, Worcestershire sauce, and cheddar cheese.

2. Spread broccoli and onion in a greased casserole dish. Top the veggies with the mayonnaise mixture.

3. Transfer this broccoli casserole to Ninja Foodi Dual Heat Air Fry Oven and close its oven door. Rotate the Ninja Foodi dial to select the "Bake" mode.

4. Press the TIME/SLICES button and again use the dial to set the cooking time to 45 minutes.

5. Now Press the TEMP/SHADE button and rotate the dial to set the temperature at 350°F.

6. Slice and serve warm.

# Feta and Vegetable Bake

Preparation Time: 15 minutes
Cooking Time: 30 minutes
Servings: 3-4

## Recipe Ingredients:

- ½ cup of brown rice, cooked
- 5 ounces of feta cheese, cubed
- 2 tablespoons of olive oil
- 2 tablespoons of basil, dried
- 2 tablespoons of parsley, dried
- 1 garlic clove
- 1 onion, julienned
- 1 bell pepper, red, julienned
- 2 good handful cherry tomatoes
- 1 jalapeño, chopped
- 1 handful olives, sliced
- 10 tablespoons of water

## Cooking Instruction:

1. Start by spreading the cheese in a SearPlate and drizzle half of the herbs on top. Toss remaining vegetables with rice and water, spread over the cheese.

2. Add remaining herbs on top and spread them evenly. Then, transfer the pan to Ninja Foodi Dual Heat Air Fry Oven and close the door.

3. Select "Bake" mode by rotating the dial. Press the TEMP/SHADE button and change the value to 350°F.

4. Press the TIME/SLICES button and change the value to 30 minutes, then press Start/Stop to begin cooking.

5. Serve warm.

# Vegan Cakes

Preparation Time: 15 minutes
Cooking Time: 15 minutes
Servings: 7-8

## Recipe Ingredients:
- 4 potatoes, diced and boiled
- 1 bunch green onions
- 1 lime, zest, and juice
- 1½-inch knob of fresh ginger
- 1 tablespoon of tamari
- 4 tablespoons of red curry paste
- 4 sheets nori
- 1 (398 grams) can heart of palm, drained
- ¾ cup of canned artichoke hearts, drained
- Black pepper, to taste
- Salt, to taste

## Cooking Instruction:

1. Add potatoes, green onions, lime zest, juice, and the rest of the ingredients to a food processor. Then, press the pulse button and blend until smooth.

2. Make 8 small patties out of this mixture. Place the patties in the air fry basket. Transfer the basket to Ninja Foodi Dual Heat Air Fry Oven and close the door.

3. Select "Air Fry" mode by rotating the dial. Press the TIME/SLICES button and change the value to 15 minutes.

4. Press the TEMP/SHADE button and change the value to 400°F. Press Start/Stop to begin cooking.

# Roast Cauliflower and Broccoli

Preparation Time: 15 minutes
Cooking Time: 10 minutes
Servings: 3-4

## Recipe Ingredients:
- ½ pound of broccoli, florets
- ½ pound of cauliflower, florets
- 1 tablespoon of olive oil
- Black pepper, to taste
- Salt, to taste
- ⅓ cup of water

## Cooking Instruction:
1. Toss all the veggies with seasoning in a large bowl. Spread these vegetables in the air fry basket.

2. Transfer the basket to Ninja Foodi Dual Heat Air Fry Oven and close the door. Select "Air Fry" mode by rotating the dial.

3. Press the TIME/SLICES button and change the value to 10 minutes. Press the TEMP/SHADE button and change the value to 400°F.

4. Press Start/Stop to begin cooking. Serve warm.

# Fried Tortellini

Preparation Time: 15 minutes
Cooking Time: 10 minutes
Servings: 7-8

## Recipe Ingredients:
- 1 (9-ounce) package cheese tortellini
- 1 cup of Panko breadcrumbs
- ⅓ cup of Parmesan, grated
- 1 teaspoon of dried oregano
- ½ teaspoon of garlic powder
- ½ teaspoon of crushed red pepper flakes
- Kosher salt, to taste
- Freshly ground black pepper, to taste
- 1 cup of all-purpose flour
- 2 large eggs

## Cooking Instruction:
1. At first, boil tortellini according to salted boiling water according to package's instructions, then drain.

2. Mix panko with garlic powder, black pepper, salt, red pepper flakes, oregano, Parmesan in a small bowl.

3. Beat eggs in a separate bowl and spread flour on a plate. Coat the tortellini with the flour, dip into the eggs and then coat with the panko mixture.

4. Then, spread the tortellini in the air fry basket and spray them with cooking oil. Transfer the basket to Ninja Foodi Dual Heat Air Fry Oven and close the door.

5. Select "Air Fry" mode by rotating the dial. Press the TIME/SLICES button and change the value to 10 minutes.

6. Press the TEMP/SHADE button and change the value to 400°F. Press Start/Stop to begin cooking.

# Cauliflower Tots

Preparation Time: 5 minutes
Cooking Time: 10 minutes
Servings: 3-4

## Recipe Ingredients:
- Cooking spray
- 450g cauliflower tots

## Cooking Instruction:
1. Start by Using a nonstick cooking spray, coat the air fry basket. Then, place as many cauliflower tots as you can in the air fry basket.

2. Ensure they do not touch, and air fry in batches if needed. Turn on Ninja Foodi Dual Heat Air Fry Oven and rotate the knob to select "Air Fry".

3. Select the timer for 6 minutes and the temperature for 400°F and allow to cook.

4. Pull the basket out, flip the tots, and cook for another 3 minutes, or until browned and cooked through.

5. Remove from Ninja Foodi Dual Heat Air Fry Oven to serve.

# Spicy Potato

Preparation Time: 15 minutes
Cooking Time: 25 minutes
Servings: 3-4

## Recipe Ingredients:
- 2 cups of water
- 6 russet potatoes, peeled and cubed
- ½ tablespoon of extra-virgin olive oil
- ½ of onion, chopped
- 1 tablespoon of fresh rosemary, chopped
- 1 garlic clove, minced
- 1 jalapeño pepper, chopped
- ½ teaspoon of garam masala powder
- ¼ teaspoon of ground cumin
- ¼ teaspoon of red chili powder
- Salt and ground black pepper, as required

## Cooking Instruction:
1. At first, In a large bowl, add the water and potatoes and set aside for about 30 minutes. Drain well and pat dry with the paper towels.

2. In another bowl, add the potatoes and oil and toss to coat well. Press AIR OVEN MODE button of Ninja Foodi Dual Heat Air Fry Oven and turn the dial to select "Air Fry" mode.

3. Press TIME/SLICES button and again turn the dial to set the cooking time to 5 minutes.

4. Now push TEMP/SHADE button and rotate the dial to set the temperature at 330°F. Press "Start/Stop" button to start.

5. When the timer is up to signal the unit is preheated, open the oven door. Arrange the potato cubes in air fry basket and insert in the oven.

6. Remove from oven and transfer the potatoes into a bowl. Add the remaining ingredients and toss to coat well.

7. Press AIR OVEN MODE button of Ninja Foodi Dual Heat Air Fry Oven and turn the dial to select "Air Fry" mode.

8. Press TIME/SLICES button and again turn the dial to set the cooking time to 20 minutes.

9. Next, push TEMP/SHADE button and rotate the dial to set the temperature at 390°F. Press "Start/Stop" button to start.

10. When the unit beeps to signal that it is preheated, open the oven door and arrange the potato mixture in air fry basket and insert in the oven.

11. When cooking time is completed, open the oven door and serve hot.

# Roasted Green Beans

Preparation Time: 5 minutes
Cooking Time: 15 minutes
Servings: 3-4

## Recipe Ingredients:
- **2 tablespoons of lard**
  - 290g whole green beans
  - 1 tablespoon of minced garlic
  - 2 tablespoons of pimentos, diced
  - Garlic powder, to taste
  - Onion powder, to taste
  - Salt, to taste

## Cooking Instruction:
1. In a stovetop pot, melt the lard. Sauté until the green beans are bright green and glossy, then add the additional ingredients.

2. Using parchment paper, line the air fry basket. Arrange the greens in a single layer on the air fry basket.

3. Turn on Ninja Foodi Dual Heat Air Fry Oven and rotate the knob to select "Air Fry".

4. Select the timer for 15 minutes and the temperature at 390°F. Remove from Ninja Foodi Dual Heat Air Fry Oven to serve.

# Veggie Rice

Preparation Time: 15 minutes
Cooking Time: 18 minutes
Servings: 1-2

## Recipe Ingredients:
- 2 cups of cooked white rice
- 1 tablespoon of vegetable oil
- 2 teaspoons of sesame oil, toasted and divided
- 1 tablespoon of water
- Salt and ground white pepper, as required
- 1 large egg, lightly beaten
- ½ cup of frozen peas, thawed
- ½ cup of frozen carrots, thawed
- 1 teaspoon of soy sauce
- 1 teaspoon of Sriracha sauce
- ½ teaspoon of sesame seeds, toasted

## Cooking Instruction:

1. In a large bowl, add the rice, vegetable oil, one teaspoon of sesame oil, water, salt, and white pepper and mix well.

2. Next, transfer rice mixture into a lightly greased SearPlate. Press AIR OVEN MODE button of Ninja Foodi Dual Heat Air Fry Oven and turn the dial to select "Air Fry" mode.

3. Press TIME/SLICES button and again turn the dial to set the cooking time to 18 minutes.

4. Now push TEMP/SHADE button and rotate the dial to set the temperature at 380°F. Press "Start/Stop" button to start.

5. When the timer is up to indicate the unit is preheated, open the oven door. Insert the SearPlate in the oven.

6. While cooking, stir the mixture once after 12 minutes. After 12 minutes of cooking, press "Start/Stop" to pause cooking.

7. Then, remove the pan from oven and place the beaten egg over rice. Again, insert the pan in the oven and press "Start/Stop" to resume cooking.

8. After 16 minutes of cooking, press "Start/Stop" to pause cooking. Remove the SearPlate from and stir in the peas and carrots.

9. Again, insert the SearPlate in the oven and press "Start/Stop" to resume cooking.

10. Meanwhile, in a separate bowl, mix together the soy sauce, Sriracha sauce, sesame seeds and the remaining sesame oil.

11. When cooking time is completed, open the oven door and transfer the rice mixture into a serving bowl.

12. Drizzle with the sauce mixture and serve.

# Stuffed Peppers

Preparation Time: 15 minutes
Cooking Time: 15 minutes
Servings: 5-6

## Recipe Ingredients:
- 6 green bell peppers
- 1 pound of lean ground beef
- 1 tablespoon of olive oil
- ¼ cup of green onion, diced
- ¼ cup of fresh parsley
- ½ teaspoon of ground sage
- ½ teaspoon of garlic salt
- 1 cup of rice, cooked
- 1 cup of marinara sauce to taste
- ¼ cup of mozzarella cheese, shredded

## Cooking Instruction:
1. Start by cooking the ground beef in a medium sized skillet until it is well done. Return the beef to the pan after draining it.

2. Mix the olive oil, green onion, parsley, sage, and salt in a large mixing bowl and add to the skillet with beef.

3. Add the cooked rice and marinara sauce in the skillet and stir this rice-beef mixture thoroughly.

4. Remove the tops off each pepper and discard the seeds. Scoop the mixture into each pepper and place it in the air fry basket.

5. Turn on Ninja Foodi Dual Heat Air Fry Oven and rotate the knob to select "Air Fry". Select the timer for 10 minutes and temperature for 355°F.

6. Dish out to serve and enjoy.

# Eggplant Parmesan

Preparation Time: 5 minutes
Cooking Time: 20 minutes
Servings: 1-2

## Recipe Ingredients:
- 1 medium eggplant
- 2 eggs, beaten
- ¼ cup of panko breadcrumbs
- 1 cup of mozzarella cheese
- 2 cups of marinara sauce
- Olive oil spray
- 2 tablespoons of parmesan cheese

## Cooking Instruction:

1. At first, peel the eggplant and cut it into ¼-inch slices. In a shallow plate, place the breadcrumbs.

2. Whisk the eggs in a small bowl. Then, dip the eggplant slices in the egg mixture gently. After that, cover both sides in breadcrumbs.

3. Fill your air fry basket with eggplant in a single layer. Using an olive oil spray, coat the tops of the slices.

4. Next, turn on Ninja Foodi Dual Heat Air Fry Oven and rotate the knob to select "Air Roast". Select the timer for 12 minutes and the temperature for 400°F.

5. Flip your eggplant slices after 8 minutes and drizzle the tops with olive oil. Allow to cook for another 4 minutes after spraying the tops of your eggplant.

6. Spread marinara sauce evenly over the top of your eggplant rounds and sprinkle with mozzarella and parmesan cheese.

7. Rotate the knob to select "Air Fry". Set the time for 3 minutes and temperature for 350°F.

# Vegetable Casserole

Preparation Time: 15 minutes
Cooking Time: 42 minutes
Servings: 5-6

## Recipe Ingredients:
- 2 cups of peas
- 8 ounces of mushrooms, sliced
- 4 tablespoons of all-purpose flour
- 1½ cups of celery, sliced
- 1½ cups of carrots, sliced
- ½ teaspoon of mustard powder
- 2 cups of milk
- Salt and black pepper, to taste
- 7 tablespoons of butter
- 1 cup of breadcrumbs
- ½ cup of Parmesan cheese, grated

## Cooking Instruction:
1. At first, grease and rub a casserole dish with butter and keep it aside. Add carrots, onion, and celery to a saucepan, then fill it with water.

2. Immediately, cover this pot and cook for 10 minutes, then stir in peas. Cook for 4 minutes, then strain the vegetables.

3. Now melt 1 tablespoon of butter in the same saucepan and toss in mushrooms to sauté. Once the mushrooms are soft, transfer them to the vegetables.

4. Next, prepare the sauce by melting 4 tablespoons of butter in a suitable saucepan. Stir in mustard and flour, then stir cook for 2 minutes.

5. Carefully pour in the milk and stir cook until thickened, then add salt and black pepper. Then, add vegetables and mushrooms to the flour milk mixture.

6. Give everything a good mix. Make sure to spread this vegetable blend in the casserole dish evenly.

7. Toss the breadcrumbs with the remaining butter and spread it on top of vegetables.

8. Top this casserole dish with cheese, and transfer the dish to Ninja Foodi Dual Heat Air Fry Oven and close the door.

9. Select "Air Fry" mode by rotating the dial. Press the TIME/SLICES button and change the value to 25 minutes.

10. Press the TEMP/SHADE button and change the value to 350°F. Press Start/Stop to begin cooking.

11. Serve warm.

# Baked Potato

Preparation Time: 5 minutes
Cooking Time: 45 minutes
Servings: 3-4

## Recipe Ingredients:
- 4 russet potatoes
- 1½ tablespoons olive oil
- 1½ tablespoons sea salt

## Cooking Instruction:
1. Poke each potato, massage it all over with olive oil and sea salt. Place the potato in the SearPlate.

2. Turn on Ninja Foodi Dual Heat Air Fry Oven and rotate the knob to select "Bake".

3. Select the timer for 40 minutes and the temperature for 350°F. Remove the baked potatoes from the Ninja Foodi.

4. Split them in half, and top them with chosen toppings!

# Roasted Vegetables

**Preparation Time:** 10 minutes
**Cooking Time:** 32 minutes
**Servings:** 5-6

## Recipe Ingredients:
- 2 medium bell peppers cored, chopped
- 2 medium carrots, peeled and sliced
- 1 small zucchini, ends trimmed, sliced
- 1 medium broccoli, florets
- ½ red onion, peeled and diced
- 2 tablespoons of olive oil
- 1½ teaspoons of Italian seasoning
- 2 garlic cloves, minced
- Salt and freshly ground black pepper
- 1 cup of grape tomatoes
- 1 tablespoon of fresh lemon juice

## Cooking Instruction:
1. Toss all the veggies with olive oil, Italian seasoning, salt, black pepper, and garlic in a large salad bowl.

2. Spread this broccoli-zucchini mixture in the SearPlate. Transfer the SearPlate to Ninja Foodi Dual Heat Air Fry Oven and close the door.

3. Select "Bake" mode by rotating the dial. Press the TIME/SLICES button and change the value to 15 minutes.

4. Press the TEMP/SHADE button and change the value to 400°F. Press Start/Stop to begin cooking.

5. Serve warm with lemon juice on top. Enjoy.

# Green Tomatoes

Preparation Time: 15 minutes
Cooking Time: 7 minutes
Servings: 3-4

## Recipe Ingredients:
- 3 green tomatoes
- ½ teaspoon of salt
- ½ cup of flour
- 2 eggs
- 1/3 cup of cornmeal
- 1/3 cup of breadcrumbs
- 1/8 teaspoon of paprika

## Cooking Instruction:
1. Begin by slicing the green tomatoes into ¼-inch slices and generously coat with salt. Allow for at least 5 minutes of resting time.

2. Put the flour in one bowl, the egg (whisked) in the second, and the cornmeal, breadcrumbs, and paprika in the third bowl to make a breading station.

3. Using a paper towel, pat green tomato slices dry, then dip each tomato slice into the flour, add the egg, and finally the cornmeal mixture, making sure the tomato slices are completely covered.

4. Place them in air fry basket in a single layer. While you turn on Ninja Foodi Dual Heat Air Fry Oven and rotate the knob to select "Air Fry".

5. Select the timer for 9 minutes and the temperature for 380°F. Cook for 7-9 minutes, flipping and spritzing with oil halfway through.

# Brussels Sprouts Gratin

Preparation Time: 15 minutes
Cooking Time: 35 minutes
Servings: 5-6

## Recipe Ingredients:
- 1 pound of Brussels sprouts
- 1 garlic clove, cut in half
- 3 tablespoons of butter, divided
- 2 tablespoons of shallots, minced
- 2 tablespoons of all-purpose flour
- Kosher salt, to taste
- Freshly ground black pepper
- 1 dash ground nutmeg
- 1 cup of milk
- ½ cup of fontina cheese, shredded
- 1 strip of bacon, cooked and crumbled
- ½ cup of fine bread crumbs

## Cooking Instruction:
1. Start by trimming the Brussels sprouts and remove their outer leaves, then slice the sprouts into quarters, rinse them under cold water.

2. Grease a gratin dish with cooking spray and rub it with garlic halves. Boil salted water in a suitable pan, then add Brussels sprouts.

3. Cook the sprouts for 3 minutes, then immediately drain. Place a suitable saucepan over medium-low heat and melt 2 tablespoons of butter in it.

4. Toss in shallots and sauté until soft, then stir in flour, nutmeg, ½ teaspoons of salt, and black pepper. Stir cook for 2 minutes.

5. Gradually add milk and a half and half cream. Mix thoroughly and add bacon along with shredded cheese. Next, fold in Brussels sprouts.

6. Transfer this mixture to the SearPlate. Toss breadcrumbs with 1 tablespoon butter and spread over. Transfer the gratin on wire rack in Ninja Foodi Dual Heat Air Fry Oven and close the door.

7. Select "Bake" mode by rotating the dial. Press the TIME/SLICES button and change the value to 25 minutes.

8. Press the TEMP/SHADE button and change the value to 350°F. Press Start/Stop to begin cooking.

9. Serve and enjoy!

# Broiled Broccoli

Preparation Time: 5 minutes
Cooking Time: 20 minutes
Servings: 3-4

## Recipe Ingredients:
- 2 heads of broccoli, diced into large chunks
- 1½ teaspoons of olive oil
- Salt and pepper, to taste

## Cooking Instruction:
1. Slice your broccoli into large chunks. Left the stems long to make sure they would not break apart.

2. Sprinkle the broccoli with 1 tablespoon of olive oil in a large mixing bowl and season to taste with salt and pepper.

3. Toss everything together to make sure the broccoli is well-coated, then place the broccoli on the SearPlate in a single layer.

4. Turn on Ninja Foodi Dual Heat Air Fry Oven and rotate the knob to select "Broil". Select the timer for 15 minutes and temperature to LOW.

5. Serve and enjoy.

# Cheesy Green Bean Casserole

Preparation Time: 10 minutes
Cooking Time: 32 minutes
Servings: 5-6

## Recipe Ingredients:

- **4 cups of green beans, cooked and chopped**
- 3 tablespoons of butter
- 8 ounces of mushrooms, sliced
- ¼ cup of onion, chopped
- 2 tablespoons of flour
- 1 teaspoon of salt
- ¼ teaspoon of ground black pepper
- 1½ cups of milk
- 2 cups of cheddar cheese, shredded
- 2 tablespoons of sour cream
- 1 cup of soft breadcrumbs
- 2 tablespoons of butter, melted
- ¼ cup of Parmesan cheese, grated
- 1 cup of french fried onions

## Cooking Instruction:

1. At first, add butter to a suitable saucepan and melt it over medium-low heat. Toss in onion and mushrooms, then sauté until soft.

2. Stir in flour, salt, and black pepper. Mix thoroughly, then slowly pour in the milk. Stir in sour cream, green beans, and cheddar cheese.

3. Then, cook until it thickens, then transfer this green bean mixture to a SearPlate and spread it evenly. Toss breadcrumbs with fried onion and butter.

4. Top the mixture with this breadcrumbs mixture. Transfer the dish to Ninja Foodi Dual Heat Air Fry Oven and close the door.

5. Select "Bake" mode by rotating the dial. Press the TIME/SLICES button and change the value to 25 minutes.

6. Press the TEMP/SHADE button and change the value to 350°F.

7. Press Start/Stop to begin cooking. Once done, serve and enjoy!

# Blue Cheese Soufflés

Preparation Time: 15 minutes
Cooking Time: 17 minutes
Servings: 3-4

## Recipe Ingredients:
- 2 ounces unsalted butter
- 1 ounce of breadcrumbs
- 1 ounce of plain flour
- 1 pinch English mustard powder
- 1 pinch of cayenne pepper
- 10 ounces of semi-skimmed milk
- 3 ounces of blue murder cheese
- 1 fresh thyme sprig, chopped
- 4 medium eggs, separated

## Cooking Instruction:
1. Grease four ramekins with butter and sprinkle with breadcrumbs. Then, melt butter in a suitable saucepan, stir in flour, cayenne, and mustard powder.

2. Mix well and cook for 1 minute, then slowly pour in the milk. Mix well until smooth, then boil the sauce. Cook for 2 minutes.

3. Stir in cheese, and mix well until melted. Add black pepper, salt, and egg yolks.
4. Beat egg whites in a separate bowl with a mixer until they make stiff peaks and add egg whites to the cheese sauce, then mix well.

5. Divide the mixture into the ramekins and transfer to Ninja Foodi Dual Heat Air Fry Oven, then close its door.

6. Select the "Bake" mode by rotating the dial. Press the TIME/SLICES button and change the value to 14 minutes.

7. Press the TEMP/SHADE button and change the value to 350°F. Press Start/Stop to begin cooking.

8. Serve warm.

## Vegetable Nachos

Preparation Time: 10 minutes
Cooking Time: 5 minutes
Servings: 2-3

### Recipe Ingredients:
- 8 ounces Tortilla chips
- ½ cup Grilled chicken
- 1 can (15 ounces) Black beans, drained, rinsed
- 1 cup White queso
- ½ cup Grape tomatoes, halved
- ⅓ cup Green onion, diced

### Cooking Instruction:
1. Use foil to line the air fry basket. Using a nonstick spray, coat the surface.

2. Assemble the nachos by layering the chips, chicken, and beans on top. Place a layer of queso on top. Add tomatoes and onions to the top.

3. Turn on Ninja Foodi Dual Heat Air Fry Oven and rotate the knob to select "Air Fry".

4. Select the timer for 5 minutes and the temperature for 355°F. Remove from Ninja Foodi Dual Heat Air Fry Oven to serve.

# Chapter 4: Fish & Seafood Recipes

## Lobster Tail Casserole

**Preparation Time:** 15 minutes
Cooking Time: 16 minutes
Servings: 5-6

## Recipe Ingredients:
- 1 pound of salmon fillets, cut into 8 equal pieces
- 16 large sea scallops
- 16 large prawns, peeled and deveined
- 8 East Coast lobster tails split in half
- ⅓ cup of butter
- ¼ cup of white wine
- ¼ cup of lemon juice
- 2 tablespoons of chopped fresh tarragon
- 2 medium garlic cloves, minced
- ½ teaspoon of paprika
- ¼ teaspoon of ground cayenne pepper

## Cooking Instruction:
1. Whisk butter with lemon juice, wine, garlic, tarragon, paprika, salt, and cayenne pepper in a small saucepan.

2. Stir cook this mixture over medium heat for 1 minute. Toss scallops, salmon fillet, and prawns in the SearPlate and pour the butter mixture on top.

3. Next, transfer the dish to Ninja Foodi Dual Heat Air Fry Oven and close the door.

4. Select "Bake" mode by rotating the dial. Press the TIME/SLICES button and change the value to 15 minutes.

5. Press the TEMP/SHADE button and change the value to 450°F. Press Start/Stop to begin cooking.

6. Serve warm.

# Baked Sardines with Garlic and Oregano

Preparation Time: 15 minutes
Cooking Time: 45 minutes
Servings: 3-4

## Recipe Ingredients:
- 2 pounds of fresh sardines
- Salt and black pepper to taste
- 2 tablespoons of Greek oregano
- 6 cloves garlic, thinly sliced
- ½ cup of olive oil
- ½ cup of freshly squeezed lemon juice
- ½ cup of water

## Cooking Instruction:
1. Mix salt, black pepper, oregano, garlic, olive oil, lemon juice, and water in SearPlate.

2. Spread the sardines in the marinade and rub well. Leave the sardines for 10 minutes to marinate.

3. Transfer the SearPlate to Ninja Foodi Dual Heat Air Fry Oven and close the door. Select "Air Fry" mode by rotating the dial.

4. Press the TIME/SLICES button and change the value to 45 minutes.

5. Press the TEMP/SHADE button and change the value to 355°F. Press Start/Stop to begin cooking.

6. Serve warm.

# Beer-Battered Fish

Preparation Time: 15 minutes
Cooking Time: 15 minutes
Servings: 3-4

## Recipe Ingredients:
- 1½ cups of all-purpose flour
- kosher salt, to taste
- ½ teaspoon Old Bay seasoning
- 1 (12-ounce) bottle lager
- 1 large egg, beaten
- 2 pounds of cod, cut into 12 pieces
- freshly ground black pepper
- vegetable oil for frying
- lemon wedges, for serving

## Cooking Instruction:
1. Mix flour with old bay, salt, egg, and beer in a bowl. Rub the cod with black pepper and salt.

2. Then, coat the codfish with the beer batter and place it in the air fry basket.

3. Transfer the basket to Ninja Foodi Dual Heat Air Fry Oven and close the door. Select "Air Fry" mode by rotating the dial.

4. Press the TIME/SLICES button and change the value to 15 minutes. Press the TEMP/SHADE button and change the value to 350°F.

5. Press Start/Stop to begin cooking.

6. Serve warm.

# Air Fried Fish Sticks

Preparation Time: 6 minutes
Cooking Time: 15 minutes
Servings: 1-2

## Recipe Ingredients:
- ½ pound of fish fillets
- ¼ teaspoon of ground black pepper, divided
- 1 egg
- ¼ cup of flour
- ½ teaspoon of salt, divided
- ½ cup of breadcrumbs, dried

## Cooking Instruction:
1. Take a bowl and add flour, salt and pepper. In a second bowl, whisk the egg. In another bowl, add breadcrumbs.

2. Then, dredge the fish in flour, then dip in egg and lastly coat with breadcrumbs.

3. Once they are done, put them in an air fry basket. Turn on your Ninja Foodi Dual Heat Air Fry Oven and rotate the knob to select "Air Fry".

4. Select the timer for about 10 to 15 minutes and temperature for 400°F.

5. Serve and enjoy!

# Baked Tilapia with Butterfly Crumb Topping

Preparation Time: 15 minutes
Cooking Time: 15 minutes
Servings: 3-4

## Recipe Ingredients:
- 4 tilapia fillets
- Salt and black pepper to taste
- 1 cup of bread crumbs
- 3 tablespoons of butter, melted
- ½ teaspoon of dried basil

## Cooking Instruction:
1. Firstly, rub the tilapia fillets with black pepper and salt, then place them in the SearPlate.

2. Mix butter, breadcrumbs, and seasonings in a bowl. Sprinkle the breadcrumbs mixture on top of the tilapia.

3. Transfer the SearPlate to Ninja Foodi Dual Heat Air Fry Oven and close the door. Select "Bake" mode by rotating the dial.

4. Press the TIME/SLICES button and change the value to 15 minutes. Press the TEMP/SHADE button and change the value to 375°F.

5. Press Start/Stop to begin cooking. Switch to "Broil" at "HI" and cook for 1 minute.

6. Serve warm.

# Fish in Yogurt Marinade

Preparation Time: 15 minutes
Cooking Time: 10 minutes
Servings: 1-2

## Recipe Ingredients:
- 1 cup of plain Greek yogurt
- Finely grated zest of 1 lemon
- 1 tablespoon of lemon juice
- 1 tablespoon of finely minced garlic
- 3 tablespoons of fresh oregano leaves
- 1 teaspoon of ground cumin
- ¼ teaspoon of ground allspice
- ½ teaspoon of salt
- ½ teaspoon of freshly ground black pepper
- 1½ pounds of perch filets

## Cooking Instruction:
1. Mix lemon zest, yogurt, garlic, cumin, oregano, black pepper, salt, and all spices in SearPlate.

2. Then, add fish to this marinade, mix well to coat then cover it with a plastic wrap. Marinate for 15 minutes in the refrigerator, then uncover.

3. Transfer the SearPlate to Ninja Foodi Dual Heat Air Fry Oven and close the door. Select "Bake" mode by rotating the dial.

4. Press the TIME/SLICES button and change the value to 10 minutes. Press the TEMP/SHADE button and change the value to 450°F.

5. Press Start/Stop to begin cooking.

6. Serve warm.

# Rum-Glazed Shrimp

Preparation Time: 10 minutes
Cooking Time: 5 minutes
Servings: 3-4

## Recipe Ingredients:
- 1½ pounds of shrimp, peeled and deveined
- 3 tablespoons of olive oil
- ⅓ cup of sweet chili sauce
- ¼ cup of soy sauce
- ¼ Captain Morgan Spiced Rum
- 2 garlic cloves, minced
- Juice of 1 lime
- ½ teaspoon of crushed red pepper flakes
- 1 green onion, thinly sliced

## Cooking Instruction:
1. Mix shrimp with all the ingredients in a bowl. Cover and marinate the shrimp for 30 minutes. Spread the glazed shrimp in a SearPlate.

2. Transfer the SearPlate to Ninja Foodi Dual Heat Air Fry Oven and close the door. Select "Bake" mode by rotating the dial.

3. Press the TIME/SLICES button and change the value to 5 minutes. Press the TEMP/SHADE button and change the value to 375°F.

4. Press Start/Stop to begin cooking.

5. Serve warm.

# Garlic Butter Salmon Bites

Preparation Time: 6 minutes
Cooking Time: 10 minutes
Servings: 1-2

## Recipe Ingredients:
- 1 tablespoon of lemon juice
- 2 tablespoons of butter
- ½ tablespoon of garlic, minced
- ½ teaspoon of pepper
- 4 ounces of salmon
- ½ teaspoon of salt
- ½ tablespoon of apple cider or rice vinegar

## Cooking Instruction:
1. Take a large bowl and add everything except salmon and whisk together until well combined.

2. Then, slice the salmon into small cubes and marinade them into the mixture. Next, cover the bowl with plastic wrap and refrigerate it for about an hour.

3. Now, spread out the marinated salmon cubes into the air fry basket. Turn on your Ninja Foodi Dual Heat Air Fry Oven and rotate the knob to select "Air Fry".

4. Select the timer for 10 minutes and temperature for 350°F. Wait till the salmon is finely cooked.

5. Serve and enjoy!

# Tilapia with Herbs and Garlic

Preparation Time: 4 minutes
Cooking Time: 10 minutes
Servings: 1-2

## Recipe Ingredients:
- 1 teaspoon of olive oil
- 1 teaspoon of fresh chives, chopped
- 1 fresh tilapia fillet
- ½ teaspoon of garlic, minced
- 1 teaspoon of fresh parsley, chopped
- Fresh ground pepper, to taste
- Salt, to taste

## Cooking Instruction:
1. Take a small bowl and add everything except the tilapia fillets and stir together.

2. Dredge tilapia fillets in the prepared mixture. Turn on your Ninja Foodi Dual Heat Air Fry Oven and rotate the knob to select "Air Fry".

3. Select the timer for about 10 minutes and temperature for 400°F Grease the air fry basket using little olive oil and place the seasoned fillets.

4. Let it cook and then serve.

# Breaded Shrimp

Preparation Time: **8 minutes**
Cooking Time: 7 minutes
Servings: 1-2

## Recipe Ingredients:
- ¼ teaspoon of garlic powder
- ¼ teaspoon of onion powder
- ¼ teaspoon of salt
- ½ pound of raw shrimp
- 1 egg
- 2 teaspoons of flour
- ½ teaspoon of corn starch
- 1 tablespoon of water
- 6 tablespoons of fine breadcrumbs
- 6 tablespoons of panko breadcrumbs

## Cooking Instruction:
1. At first, take a small bowl, add flour, corn starch, garlic powder, onion powder and salt. Add shrimp in the bowl.

2. Toss to coat well. In a second bowl, whisk in the egg. Mix the panko breadcrumbs and fine breadcrumbs together in another bowl.

3. Now, take seasoned shrimp, dip in the egg and place in the breadcrumbs mixture. Lightly grease the air fry basket.

4. Turn on your Ninja Foodi Dual Heat Air Fry Oven and rotate the knob to select "Air Fry". Select the timer for about 7 minutes and temperature for 370°F.

5. Place the coated shrimp to the air fry basket and let it cook.

6. Serve and enjoy!

# Air Fried Fish Cakes

Preparation Time: 5 minutes
Cooking Time: 10 minutes
Servings: 1-2

## Recipe Ingredients:
- ½ pound of white fish, finely chopped
- 1/3 cup of panko breadcrumbs
- 2 tablespoons of cilantro, chopped
- 1 tablespoon of chili sauce
- Cooking spray
- ½ egg
- 1 tablespoon of mayonnaise
- 1/8 teaspoon of ground pepper
- 1 pinch of salt

## Cooking Instruction:
1. Take a bowl and add all ingredients together until well combined. Shape the mixture into cakes.

2. Grease the air fry basket using cooking spray. Turn on your Ninja Foodi Dual Heat Air Fry Oven and rotate the knob to select "Air Fry".

3. Select the timer for about 10 minutes and temperature for 400 °F. Let the fish cakes cook until they are golden brown.

4. Serve and enjoy!

# Lobster Tails with Lemon-Garlic Butter

Preparation Time: 5 minutes
Cooking Time: 10 minutes
Servings: 1-2

## Recipe Ingredients:
- 2 tablespoons butter
- ½ teaspoon lemon zest
- 1 lobster tail
- ½ clove garlic, grated
- ½ teaspoon parsley, chopped
- Salt, to taste
- Fresh ground black pepper, to taste

## Cooking Instruction:
1. Cut the lobster tail lengthwise through the center of the hard-top shell. Cut to the bottom of the shell and spread the tail halves apart.

2. Place the lobster tail in the air fry basket. Take a saucepan and melt butter on medium heat. Add garlic and lemon zest and cook for 30 seconds.

3. Now, pour the butter mixture onto lobster tail. Turn on your Ninja Foodi Dual Heat Air Fry Oven and rotate the knob to select "Air Fry".

4. Select the timer for about 5 to 7 minutes and temperature for 380°F. Let it cook and serve with parsley as topping.

# Fish Casserole

Preparation Time: 10 minutes
Cooking Time: 40 minutes
Servings: 2-3

## Recipe Ingredients:
- ½ tablespoon of unsalted butter, softened
- ¼ teaspoon of salt
- 1 pound of white fish fillet
- ¼ teaspoon of pepper
- ½ sweet onion, thinly sliced
- 2 teaspoons of extra-virgin olive oil, divided
- ¼ teaspoon of dry thyme
- 1 pinch nutmeg
- 1 bread slice, crusts removed
- ¼ teaspoon of paprika
- 1/8 teaspoon of garlic powder
- ½ cup of shredded Swiss cheese

## Cooking Instruction:
1. Turn on your Ninja Foodi Dual Heat Air Fry Oven and rotate the knob to select "Bake". Preheat by selecting the timer for 3 minutes and temperature for 400°F.

2. Then, arrange fish fillet on a dish and season with salt and pepper. Take a pan and heat oil over medium-high heat.

3. Add onion and cook until it starts to brown. Stir in thyme and nutmeg. Spread the onion mixture over fish.

4. In a food processor, add bread slice, paprika, garlic powder and a little oil. Process until we have a moist mixture. Sprinkle crumbs over the onion mixture.

5. Add cheese on top of casserole and place inside Ninja Foodi Dual Heat Air Fry Oven. Select the timer for about 18 to 22 minutes and temperature for 400°F.

6. Serve warm.

# Scallops with Chanterelles

Preparation Time: 10 minutes
Cooking Time: 15 minutes
Servings: 2-3

## Recipe Ingredients:
- 1 tablespoon of balsamic vinegar
- ½ pound of scallops
- 3 tablespoons of butter
- ½ tomato, peeled, seeded, and chopped
- 1 tablespoon of butter
- ¼ pound of chanterelle mushrooms

## Cooking Instruction:
1. Take a pan and add half tablespoon butter over medium heat. Stir in chanterelles and cook for 5 to 8 minutes.

2. Transfer to a bowl. Add remaining butter in the same pan over low heat and cook for 5 minutes.

3. Stir in tomato and balsamic vinegar and cook for 2 minutes. Stir the tomato mixture into mushrooms.

4. Transfer the tomato-mushroom mixture into SearPlate. Turn on your Ninja Foodi Dual Heat Air Fry Oven and rotate the knob to select "Broil".

5. Next, select the timer for about 2 minutes per side and set the temperature to HI.

6. When the unit beeps to signify it has preheated, insert the SearPlate in the oven. Close the oven and let it cook.

7. Serve warm and enjoy!

# Crispy Flounder

Preparation Time: 15 minutes
Cooking Time: 12 minutes
Servings: 2-3

## Recipe Ingredients:
- 1 egg
- 1 cup dry Italian breadcrumb
- ¼ cup olive oil
- 3 (6-ounce) flounder fillets

## Cooking Instruction:
1. In a shallow bowl, beat the egg. In another bowl, add the breadcrumbs and oil and mix until a crumbly mixture is formed.

2. Next, dip the flounder fillets into the beaten egg and then coat with the breadcrumb mixture.

3. Press AIR OVEN MODE button of Ninja Foodi Dual Heat Air Fry Oven and turn the dial to select "Air Fry" mode.

4. Press TIME/SLICES button and again turn the dial to set the cooking time to 12 minutes.

5. Now push TEMP/SHADE button and rotate the dial to set the temperature at 355°F. Press "Start/Stop" button to start.

6. When the unit beeps to show that it is preheated, open the oven door and grease the air fry basket.

7. Place the flounder fillets into the prepared air fry basket and insert in the oven. When cooking time is completed, open the oven door.

8. Serve hot.

# Prawns in Butter Sauce

**Preparation Time:** 15 minutes
**Cooking Time:** 6 minutes
Servings: 1-2

## Recipe Ingredients:
- ½ pound of large prawns, peeled and deveined
- 1 large garlic clove, minced
- 1 tablespoon of butter, melted
- 1 teaspoon of fresh lemon zest, grated

## Cooking Instruction:
1. In a bowl, add all the ingredients and toss to coat well. Set aside at room temperature for about 30 minutes.

2. Arrange the prawn mixture into a SearPlate. Press AIR OVEN MODE button of Ninja Foodi Dual Heat Air Fry Oven and turn the dial to select "Bake" mode.

3. Press TIME/SLICES button and again turn the dial to set the cooking time to 6 minutes.

4. Now push TEMP/SHADE button and rotate the dial to set the temperature at 450°F. Press "Start/Stop" button to start.

5. When the unit beeps to show that it is preheated, open the oven door. Insert the SearPlate in the oven. Close the oven and let it cook.

6. When cooking time is completed, open the oven door and serve immediately.

# Fish Newburg with Haddock

Preparation Time: 15 minutes
Cooking Time: 29 minutes
Servings: 3-4

## Recipe Ingredients:

- 1½ pounds of haddock fillets
- Salt and freshly ground black pepper
- 4 tablespoons of butter
- 1 tablespoon & 2 teaspoons of flour
- ¼ teaspoon of sweet paprika
- ¼ teaspoon of ground nutmeg
- Dash cayenne pepper
- ¾ cup of heavy cream
- ½ cup of milk
- 3 tablespoons of dry sherry
- 2 large egg yolks
- 4 pastry shells

## Cooking Instruction:

1. Rub haddock with black pepper and salt, then place in a SearPlate. Place the spiced haddock in the pastry shell and close it like a calzone.

2. Drizzle 1 tablespoon of melted butter on top. Transfer the SearPlate to Ninja Foodi Dual Heat Air Fry Oven and close the door.

3. Select "Bake" mode by rotating the dial. Press the TIME/SLICES button and change the value to 25 minutes. Press the TEMP/SHADE button.

4. Change the value to 350°F. Press Start/Stop to begin cooking. Meanwhile, melt 3 tablespoons of butter in a suitable saucepan over low heat. Stir in nutmeg, cayenne, paprika, and salt, then mix well.

5. Add flour to the spice butter and whisk well to avoid lumps. Cook for 2 minutes, then add milk and cream. Mix well and cook until thickens.

6. Beat egg yolks with sherry in a bowl and stir in a ladle of cream mixture. Mix well and return the mixture to the saucepan.

7. Cook the mixture on low heat for 2 minutes. Add the baked wrapped haddock to the sauce and cook until warm. Serve warm.

# Seafood Medley Mix

Preparation Time: 5 minutes
Cooking Time: 15 minutes
Servings: 1-2

## Recipe Ingredients:
- ½ pound of frozen seafood medley
- Oil or cooking spray
- Salt and black pepper, to taste

## Cooking Instruction:
1. Take an air fry basket and evenly spray with a cooking spray. Put frozen seafood medley in the air fry basket.

2. Turn on your Ninja Foodi Dual Heat Air Fry Oven and rotate the knob to select "Air Fry".

3. Select the timer for 15 minutes and temperature for 400°F. Season the seafood medley with salt and pepper.

4. Serve and enjoy!

# Buttered Crab Shells

Preparation Time: 15 minutes
Cooking Time: 20 minutes
Servings: 3-4

## Recipe Ingredients:
- 4 soft crab shells, cleaned
- 1 cup of buttermilk
- 3 eggs
- 2 cups of panko breadcrumb
- 2 teaspoons of seafood seasoning
- 1½ teaspoons of lemon zest, grated
- 2 tablespoons of butter, melted

## Cooking Instruction:
1. In a shallow bowl, place the buttermilk. In a second bowl, whisk the eggs. In a third bowl, mix together the breadcrumbs, seafood seasoning, and lemon zest.

2. Soak the crab shells into the buttermilk for about 10 minutes. Now, dip the crab shells into beaten eggs and then, coat with the breadcrumb mixture.

3. Press AIR OVEN MODE button of Ninja Foodi Dual Heat Air Fry Oven and turn the dial to select "Air Fry" mode.

4. Press TIME/SLICES button and again turn the dial to set the cooking time to 10 minutes. Now push TEMP/SHADE button and rotate the dial to set the temperature at 375°F.

5. Press "Start/Stop" button to start. When the unit beeps to show that it is preheated, open the oven door and grease the air fry basket.

6. Then, place the crab shells into the prepared air fry basket and insert in the oven. When cooking time is completed, open the oven door.

7. Transfer the crab shells onto serving plates. Drizzle crab shells with the melted butter and serve immediately.

# Scallops with Capers Sauce

Preparation Time: 10 minutes
Cooking Time: 6 minutes
Servings: 1-2

## Recipe Ingredients:
- 10 (1-ounce) sea scallops, cleaned and patted very dry
- Salt and ground black pepper, as required
- ¼ cup of extra-virgin olive oil
- 2 tablespoons of fresh parsley, finely chopped
- 2 teaspoons of capers, finely chopped
- 1 teaspoon of fresh lemon zest, finely grated
- ½ teaspoon of garlic, finely chopped

## Cooking Instruction:
1. Season each scallop evenly with salt and black pepper. Press AIR OVEN MODE button of Ninja Foodi Dual Heat Air Fry Oven.

2. Turn the dial to select "Air Fry" mode. Press TIME/SLICES button and again turn the dial to set the cooking time to 6 minutes.

3. Now push TEMP/SHADE button and rotate the dial to set the temperature at 400°F. Press "Start/Stop" button to start.

4. When the unit beeps to show that it is preheated, open the oven door and grease the air fry basket. Then, place the scallops into the prepared air fry basket.

5. Insert in the oven. Meanwhile, for the sauce: in a bowl, mix the remaining ingredients. When cooking time is completed, open the oven door.

6. Transfer the scallops onto serving plates. Top with the sauce and serve immediately.

# Scallops with Spinach

Preparation Time: 15 minutes
Cooking Time: 10 minutes
Servings: 1-2

## Recipe Ingredients:
- ¾ cup of heavy whipping cream
- 1 tablespoon of tomato paste
- 1 teaspoon of garlic, minced
- 1 tablespoon of fresh basil, chopped
- Salt and ground black pepper, as required
- 8 jumbo sea scallops
- Olive oil cooking spray
- 1 (12-ounce) package frozen spinach, thawed and drained

## Cooking Instruction:

1. In a bowl, place the cream, tomato paste, garlic, basil, salt, and black pepper and mix well. Spray each scallop evenly with cooking spray.

2. Sprinkle with a little salt and black pepper. In the bottom of a baking pan, place the spinach. Arrange scallops on top of the spinach on SearPlate in a single layer.

3. Top with the cream mixture evenly. Press AIR OVEN MODE button of Ninja Foodi Dual Heat Air Fry Oven and turn the dial to select "Air Fry" mode.

4. Press TIME/SLICES button and again turn the dial to set the cooking time to 10 minutes. Now push TEMP/SHADE button and rotate the dial to set the temperature at 350°F.

5. Press "Start/Stop" button to start. When the unit beeps to show that it is preheated, open the oven door. Place the SearPlate in the oven.

6. When cooking time is completed, open the oven door and serve hot.

# Shrimp Fajitas

Preparation Time: 5 minutes
Cooking Time: 10 minutes
Servings: 1-2

## Recipe Ingredients:
- ½ pound of raw shrimp
- ½ small onion, sliced
- ½ tablespoon of vegetable oil, divided
- ½ tablespoon of fajita seasoning
- 1 red bell pepper, sliced
- 1 green bell pepper, sliced

## Cooking Instruction:
1. Take a bowl and season the vegetables. Add half of the oil and fajita seasoning. Turn on your Ninja Foodi Dual Heat Air Fry Oven.

2. Rotate the knob to select "Air Fry". Select the timer for 3 minutes and temperature for 375°F. Air fry the vegetable.

3. Meanwhile season the shrimp with rest of oil and fajita seasoning. After 3 minutes add the seasoned shrimp to the side.

4. Now, air fry for another 6 minutes at the same temperature.

5. Serve and enjoy!

# Seafood Casserole

Preparation Time: 15 minutes
Cooking Time: 20 minutes
Servings: 7-8

## Recipe Ingredients:
- 8 ounces haddock, skinned and diced
- 1 pound of scallops
- 1 pound of large shrimp, peeled and deveined
- 3 to 4 garlic cloves, minced
- ½ cup of heavy cream
- ½ cup of Swiss cheese, shredded
- 2 tablespoons of Parmesan, grated
- Paprika, to taste
- Sea salt and black pepper, to taste

## Cooking Instruction:
1. Grease the SearPlate with cooking spray. Toss shrimp, scallops, and haddock chunks in the greased SearPlate.

2. Drizzle salt, black pepper, and minced garlic over the seafood mix. Top this seafood with cream, Swiss cheese, paprika, and Parmesan cheese.

3. Transfer the dish to the Ninja Digital Air Fryer Oven and close its oven door. Select "Bake" mode by rotating the dial.

4. Press the TIME/SLICES button and change the value to 20 minutes. Press the TEMP/SHADE button and change the value to 375°F.

5. Press Start/Stop to begin cooking. Serve warm.

# Lemon Pepper Shrimp

Preparation Time: 5 minutes
Cooking Time: 8 minutes
Servings: 3-4

## Recipe Ingredients:
- 2 lemons, juiced
- ½ tablespoon of lemon pepper
- 2 tablespoons of olive oil
- ½ teaspoon of paprika
- ½ teaspoon of garlic powder
- 1½ pounds of shrimp

## Cooking Instruction:

1. Take a bowl, add all the ingredients together and mix well. Add shrimp and toss to coat well.

2. Turn on your Ninja Foodi Dual Heat Air Fry Oven and rotate the knob to select "Air Fry".

3. Select the timer for about 6 to 8 minutes and temperature for 400°F. Place shrimp in the air fry basket and cook until pink.

4. Serve and enjoy!

# Spicy Bay Scallops

Preparation Time: 15 minutes
Cooking Time: 8 minutes
Servings: 3-4

## Recipe Ingredients:
- 1 pound of bay scallops rinsed and patted dry
- 2 teaspoons of smoked paprika
- 2 teaspoons of chili powder
- 2 teaspoons of olive oil
- 1 teaspoon of garlic powder
- ¼ teaspoon of ground black pepper
- ⅛ teaspoon of cayenne red pepper

## Cooking Instruction:
1. Scallops with paprika, chili powder, olive oil, garlic powder, black pepper, and red pepper in a bowl.

2. Place the scallops in the air fry basket. Transfer the basket to Ninja Foodi Dual Heat Air Fry Oven and close the door.

3. Select "Air Fry" mode by rotating the dial. Press the TIME/SLICES button and change the value to 8 minutes.

4. Press the TEMP/SHADE button and change the value to 400°F. Press Start/Stop to begin cooking. Enjoy.

# Maple Bacon Salmon

Preparation Time: 15 minutes
Cooking Time: 29 minutes
Servings: 3-4

## Recipe Ingredients:

**Salmon**
- 1 lemon, sliced
- 1 (2 ¼-pound) skin-on salmon fillet
- 2 ½ teaspoons of salt, black pepper, and garlic seasoning
- 1 tablespoon of Dijon mustard
- ⅓ cup of olive oil
- 2 tablespoons of lemon juice
- 2 tablespoons of maple syrup
- Chopped chives for garnish

**Candied Bacon**
- 3 tablespoons of maple syrup
- 1 tablespoon of packed brown sugar
- ¼ teaspoon of salt, black pepper and garlic seasoning

## Cooking Instruction:

1. Place lemon slices in the SearPlate and top them with salmon. Drizzle salt, black pepper, and garlic seasoning on top.

2. Mix mustard, oil, maple syrup, lemon juice, salt, black pepper, and seasoning in a bowl. Pour this sauce over the salmon.

3. Transfer the SearPlate to Ninja Foodi Dual Heat Air Fry Oven and close the door. Select "Air Fry" mode by rotating the dial.

4. Press the TIME/SLICES button and change the value to 25 minutes. Press the TEMP/SHADE button and change the value to 350°F.

5. Press Start/Stop to begin cooking. Meanwhile, mix brown sugar, salt, black pepper, and garlic seasoning in a bowl.

6. Sauté bacon in a skillet until crispy and pour the sugar syrup on top. Cook for 4 minutes until the liquid is absorbed.

7. Allow the bacon to cool and then crumble it. Garnish the salmon with crumbled bacon and chopped chives.

8. Serve warm.

# Chapter 5: Poultry Recipes

## Creamy Chicken Casserole

**Preparation Time:** 15 minutes
Cooking Time: 47 minutes
Servings: 3-4

### Recipe Ingredients:
**Chicken Mushroom Casserole**
- 2½ pounds of chicken breasts, cut into strips
- 1½ teaspoons of salt
- ¼ teaspoon of black pepper
- 1 cup all-purpose flour
- 6 tablespoons of olive oil
- 1 pound of white mushrooms, sliced
- 1 medium onion, diced
- 3 garlic cloves, minced

## Sauce
- 3 tablespoons of unsalted butter
- 3 tablespoons of all-purpose flour
- ½ cup of milk, optional
- 1 cups of chicken broth, optional
- 1 tablespoon of lemon juice
- 1 cup of half and half cream

### Cooking Instruction:
1. Butter a casserole dish and toss in chicken with mushrooms and all the casserole ingredients. Then, prepare the sauce in a suitable pan.

2. Add butter and melt over moderate heat. Stir in all-purpose flour and whisk well for 2 minutes, then pour in milk, chicken broth, lemon juice, and cream.

3. Mix well and pour this creamy white sauce over the chicken mix in the SearPlate. Transfer the SearPlate to Ninja Foodi Dual Heat Air Fry Oven and close the door.

4. Select "Bake" mode by rotating the dial. Press the TIME/SLICES button and change the value to 45 minutes.

5. Press the TEMP/SHADE button and change the value to 350°F. Press Start/Stop to begin cooking. Serve warm.

## Duck a la Orange

Preparation Time: 15 minutes
Cooking Time: 60 minutes
Servings: 7-8

### Recipe Ingredients:
- 1 tablespoon of salt
- 1 teaspoon of ground coriander
- ½ teaspoon of ground cumin
- 1 teaspoon of black pepper
- 1 (5- to 6-pound) duck, skinned
- 1 juice orange, halved
- 4 fresh thyme sprigs
- 4 fresh marjoram sprigs
- 2 parsley sprigs
- 1 small onion, cut into wedges
- ½ cup of dry white wine
- ½ cup of chicken broth
- ½ carrot
- ½ celery rib

### Cooking Instruction:
1. Place the Pekin duck in a SearPlate and whisk orange juice and the rest of the ingredients in a bowl.

2. Pour the herb sauce over the duck and brush it liberally. Transfer the SearPlate to Ninja Foodi Dual Heat Air Fry Oven and close the door.

3. Select "Air Fry" mode by rotating the dial. Press the TIME/SLICES button and change the value to 60 minutes.

4. Press the TEMP/SHADE button and change the value to 350°F. Press Start/Stop to begin cooking. Continue basting the duck during baking.

5. Serve warm.

# Baked Duck

Preparation Time: 15 minutes
Cooking Time: 2 hours 20 minutes
Servings: 3-4

## Recipe Ingredients:
- 1½ sprigs fresh rosemary
- ½ nutmeg
- Black pepper
- Juice from 1 orange
- 1 whole duck
- 4 cloves garlic, chopped
- 1½ red onions, chopped
- a few stalks celery
- 1½ carrot
- 2 cm piece fresh ginger
- 1½ bay leaves
- 2 pounds of Piper potatoes
- 4 cups of chicken stock

## Cooking Instruction:
1. Place duck in a large cooking pot and add broth along with all the ingredients.

2. Cook this duck for 2 hours on a simmer, transfer to the SearPlate, then transfer the SearPlate to Ninja Foodi Dual Heat Air Fry Oven and close the door.

3. Select "Air Fry" mode by rotating the dial. Press the TIME/SLICES button and change the value to 20 minutes.

4. Press the TEMP/SHADE button and change the value to 350°F. Press Start/Stop to begin cooking.

5. Serve warm.

# Spiced Roasted Chicken

Preparation Time: 10 minutes
Cooking Time: 1 hour
Servings: 2-3

## Recipe Ingredients:
- 1 teaspoon of paprika
- ½ teaspoon of cayenne pepper
- ½ teaspoon of ground white pepper
- ½ teaspoon of garlic powder
- 1 teaspoon of dried thyme
- ½ teaspoon of onion powder
- Salt and black pepper, to taste
- 2 tablespoons of oil
- ½ whole chicken, necks and giblets removed

## Cooking Instruction:
1. Take a bowl and mix together the thyme and spices. Coat the chicken with oil and rub it with the spice mixture.

2. Turn on your Ninja Foodi Dual Heat Air Fry Oven and rotate the knob to select "Air Fry".

3. Select the timer for about 30 minutes and temperature for 350°F. Place the chicken in the air fry basket and air fry for 30 minutes.

4. After that, take out the chicken, flip it over and let it air fry for another 30 minutes. When cooked, let it sit for 10 minutes on a large plate.

5. Carve to desired pieces. Serve and enjoy!

# Spicy Chicken Legs

Preparation Time: 20 minutes
Cooking Time: 25 minutes
Servings: 5-6

## Recipe Ingredients:
- 6 chicken legs
- 4 cups of white flour
- 2 cups of buttermilk
- 2 teaspoons of onion powder
- 2 teaspoons of garlic powder
- 2 teaspoons of paprika
- 2 teaspoons of ground cumin
- Salt and black pepper, to taste
- 2 tablespoons of olive oil

## Cooking Instruction:
1. At first, take a bowl, add chicken legs and buttermilk. Refrigerate for about 2 hours. Take another bowl, mix together flour and spices.

2. Remove the chicken legs from buttermilk and coat them with the flour mixture. Do it again until we have a fine coating.

3. Turn on your Ninja Foodi Dual Heat Air Fry Oven and rotate the knob to select "Air Fry".

4. Select the timer for about 20 to 25 minutes and temperature for 360°F. Grease the air fry basket and arrange the chicken legs on it.

5. Take it out when chicken legs are brown enough.

6. Serve onto a serving platter.

# Gingered Chicken Drumsticks

Preparation Time: 20 minutes
Cooking Time: 25 minutes
Servings: 5-6

## Recipe Ingredients:
- 4 teaspoons of fresh ginger, minced
- 4 teaspoons of galangal, minced
- ½ cup of full-fat coconut milk
- 4 teaspoons of ground turmeric
- Salt, to taste
- 6 chicken drumsticks

## Cooking Instruction:
1. At first, take a bowl and mix together galangal, ginger, coconut milk and spices. Add chicken drumsticks to the bowl for well coating.

2. Refrigerate for at least 6 to 8 hours. Turn on your Ninja Foodi Dual Heat Air Fry Oven and rotate the knob to select "Air Fry".

3. Select the timer for about 20 to 25 minutes and temperature for 375°F. Grease the air fry basket and place the drumsticks into the prepared basket.

4. Remove from the oven and serve on a platter.

5. Serve hot and enjoy!

# Sweet and Spicy Chicken Drumsticks

Preparation Time: 10 minutes
Cooking Time: 20 minutes
Servings: 1-2

## Recipe Ingredients:
- 2 chicken drumsticks
- ½ garlic clove, crushed
- 1 teaspoon of ginger, crushed
- 1 teaspoon of brown sugar
- ½ tablespoon of mustard
- ½ teaspoon of red chili powder
- ½ teaspoon of cayenne pepper
- ½ tablespoon of vegetable oil
- Salt and black pepper, to taste

## Cooking Instruction:

1. Take a bowl and mix together mustard, ginger, brown sugar, oil and spices. Add chicken drumsticks to the bowl for well coating.

2. Refrigerate for at least 20 to 30 minutes. Turn on your Ninja Foodi Dual Heat Air Fry Oven and rotate the knob to select "Air Fry".

3. Select the timer for about 10 minutes and temperature for 390°F. Grease the air fry basket and place the drumsticks into the prepared basket.

4. Air fry for about 10 minutes and then 10 more minutes at 300°F. Remove from the oven and serve on a platter.

5. Serve hot and enjoy!

# Honey-Glazed Chicken Drumsticks

Preparation Time: 10 minutes
Cooking Time: 22 minutes
Servings: 1-2

## Recipe Ingredients:
- ½ tablespoon of fresh thyme, minced
- 2 tablespoons of Dijon mustard
- ½ tablespoon of honey
- 1 tablespoon of olive oil
- 1 teaspoon of fresh rosemary, minced
- 2 chicken drumsticks, boneless
- Salt and black pepper, to taste

## Cooking Instruction:
1. Take a bowl and mix together mustard, honey, herbs, salt, oil and black pepper. Add chicken drumsticks to the bowl.

2. Coat them well with the mixture. Cover and refrigerate overnight. Turn on your Ninja Foodi Dual Heat Air Fry Oven and rotate the knob to select "Air Fry".

3. Select the timer for about 12 minutes and temperature for 320°F. Grease the air fry basket and place the drumsticks into the prepared basket.

4. Air fry for about 12 minutes and then for about 10 more minutes at 355°F. Remove from the oven and serve on a platter.

5. Serve hot and enjoy!

# Sweet and Sour Chicken Thighs

Preparation Time: 10 minutes
Cooking Time: 20 minutes
Servings: 1-2

## Recipe Ingredients:
- ¼ tablespoon of soy sauce
- ¼ tablespoon of rice vinegar
- ½ teaspoon of sugar
- ½ garlic, minced
- ½ scallion, finely chopped
- ¼ cup of corn flour
- 1 chicken thigh, skinless and boneless
- Salt and black pepper, to taste

## Cooking Instruction:

1. Take a bowl and mix all the ingredients together except chicken and corn flour. Add the chicken thigh to the bowl to coat well.

2. Take another bowl and add corn flour, then remove the chicken thighs from marinade and lightly coat with corn flour.

3. Turn on your Ninja Foodi Dual Heat Air Fry Oven and rotate the knob to select "Air Fry". Select the timer for about 10 minutes and temperature for 390°F.

4. Grease the air fry basket and place the chicken thighs into the prepared basket. Air fry for about 10 minutes and then for another to 10 minutes at 355°F.

5. Remove from the oven and serve on a platter.

6. Serve hot and enjoy!

# Herb Butter Chicken

Preparation Time: 10 minutes
Cooking Time: 15 minutes
Servings: 1-2

## Recipe Ingredients:
- 1½ cloves garlic, minced
- ½ teaspoon of dried parsley
- ⅛ teaspoon of dried rosemary
- ⅛ teaspoon of dried thyme
- 2 skinless, boneless chicken breast halves
- ¼ cup of butter, softened

## Cooking Instruction:
1. Turn on your Ninja Foodi Dual Heat Air Fry Oven and rotate the knob to select "Broil".

2. Then, cover the SearPlate with aluminum foil then carefully place chicken on it.

3. Take a small bowl and mix together parsley, rosemary, thyme, butter and garlic. Spread the mixture on top of chicken.

4. Broil in the oven with the coating of butter and herbs for at least 30 minutes at LO.

5. Serve warm and enjoy!

# Breaded Chicken Tenderloins

Preparation Time: 10 minutes
Cooking Time: 15 minutes
Servings: 1-2

## Recipe Ingredients:
- 4 chicken tenderloins, skinless and boneless
- ½ egg, beaten
- 1 tablespoon of vegetable oil
- ¼ cup of breadcrumbs

## Cooking Instruction:
1. At first, take a shallow dish and add the beaten egg. Take another dish and mix together oil and breadcrumbs until you have a crumbly mixture.

2. Dip the chicken tenderloins into the beaten egg and then coat with the bread crumbs mixture. Shake off the excess coating.

3. Turn on your Ninja Foodi Dual Heat Air Fry Oven and rotate the knob to select "Air Fry".

4. Select the timer for about 15 minutes and temperature for 355°F. Grease the air fry basket and place the chicken tenderloins into the prepared basket.

5. Remove from the oven and serve on a platter.

6. Serve hot and enjoy!

# Parmesan Chicken Bake

Preparation Time: 10 minutes
Cooking Time: 50 minutes
Servings: 2-3

## Recipe Ingredients:
- 3 skinless, boneless chicken breast halves
- 1 cup of prepared marinara sauce
- ¼ cup of grated Parmesan cheese, divided
- ½ package garlic croutons
- ½ package shredded mozzarella cheese, divided
- 2 tablespoons of chopped fresh basil
- 1 tablespoon of olive oil
- 1 clove garlic, crushed and finely chopped
- Red pepper flakes, to taste

## Cooking Instruction:
1. Turn on your Ninja Foodi Dual Heat Air Fry Oven and rotate the knob to select "Bake".

2. Preheat by selecting the timer for 3 minutes and temperature for 350°F. Grease the SearPlate and sprinkle garlic and red pepper flakes.

3. Arrange the chicken breasts on SearPlate and pour marinara sauce over chicken.

4. Then, top with half of the mozzarella cheese and Parmesan cheese and then sprinkle the croutons.

5. Add remaining mozzarella cheese on top, followed by half the Parmesan cheese.

6. Select the timer for about 50 minutes and temperature for 160°F. Bake until cheese and croutons are golden brown and the chicken is no longer pink inside.

7. Serve and enjoy!

# Chicken Alfredo Bake

Preparation Time: 8 minutes
Cooking Time: 25 minutes
Servings: 1-2

## Recipe Ingredients:
- ¼ cup of heavy cream
- ½ cup of milk
- 1 tablespoon of flour, divided
- ½ clove garlic, minced
- 1 cup of penne pasta
- ½ tablespoon of butter
- ½ cup of cubed rotisserie chicken
- ½ cup of Parmigiano-Reggiano cheese, freshly grated
- ½ pinch ground nutmeg

## Cooking Instruction:
1. Take a large pot of lightly salted water and bring it to a boil. Add penne and cook for about 11 minutes.

2. Turn on your Ninja Foodi Dual Heat Air Fry Oven and rotate the knob to select "Bake". Set time to 10 to 12 minutes and temperature to 375°F.

3. Press Start/Stop to begin preheating. Meanwhile, take a saucepan and melt butter over medium heat and cook garlic for about a minute.

4. Add in flour and whisk continuously until you have a paste. Pour in milk and cream, whisking continuously. Stir in cheese and nutmeg.

5. Now add drained penne pasta and cooked chicken. Pour the mixture into an oven-safe dish. Sprinkle cheese on top.

6. When the unit beeps to signify that it is preheated, add the dish on wire rack into Ninja Foodi Dual Heat Air Fry Oven.

7. Bake in the preheated Ninja Foodi Dual Heat Air Fry Oven for about 10 to 12 minutes at 375°F.

8. Serve and enjoy!

# Marinated Ranch Broiled Chicken

Preparation Time: 5 minutes
Cooking Time: 15 minutes
Servings: 1-2

## Recipe Ingredients:
- 1 tablespoon olive oil
- ½ tablespoon red wine vinegar
- 2 tablespoons dry Ranch-style dressing mix
- 1 chicken breast half, skinless and boneless

## Cooking Instruction:
1. Take a bowl and mix together dressing mix, oil and vinegar. Add chicken in it and toss to coat well. Refrigerate for about an hour.

2. Turn on your Ninja Foodi Dual Heat Air Fry Oven and rotate the knob to select "Broil". Set timer for 15 minutes and temperature level to HI.

3. Press Start/Stop button to begin preheating. When the unit beeps to signify that it is preheated, place chicken onto the SearPlate.

4. Broil for about 15 minutes until chicken is cooked through.

5. Serve warm and enjoy!

# Cheesy Chicken Cutlets

Preparation Time: 10 minutes
Cooking Time: 30 minutes
Servings: 1-2

## Recipe Ingredients:
- 1 large egg
- 6 tablespoons flour
- ¾ cup panko breadcrumbs
- 2 tablespoons parmesan cheese, grated
- 2 chicken cutlets, skinless and boneless
- ½ tablespoon mustard powder
- Salt and black pepper, to taste

## Cooking Instruction:
1. Take a shallow bowl, add the flour. In a separate bowl, crack the egg and beat well.

2. Take a third bowl and mix together breadcrumbs, cheeses, mustard powder, salt and black pepper. Season the chicken with salt and black pepper.

3. Coat the chicken with flour, then dip into beaten egg and then finally coat with the breadcrumbs mixture.

4. Turn on your Ninja Foodi Dual Heat Air Fry Oven and rotate the knob to select "Air Fry".

5. Select the timer for about 30 minutes and temperature for 355°F. Grease the air fry basket and place the chicken cutlets into the prepared basket.

6. Remove from the oven and serve on a platter.

7. Serve hot and enjoy!

# Lemon-Lime Chicken

Preparation Time: 10 minutes
Cooking Time: 20 minutes
Servings: 1-2

## Recipe Ingredients:
- 2 tablespoons of vegetable oil
- 2 tablespoons of lime juice
- ¼ cup of lemon juice
- 2 skinless, boneless chicken breast halves
- Italian seasoning to taste
- Salt to taste

## Cooking Instruction:
1. At first, take a large bowl and add lemon juice, lime juice and oil. Place the chicken in the mixture and refrigerate for at least an hour.

2. Turn on your Ninja Foodi Dual Heat Air Fry Oven and rotate the knob to select "Broil". Take a SearPlate.

3. Arrange the chicken on the SearPlate and season with Italian seasoning and salt.

4. Broil chicken for 10 minutes and set temperature level to LO. Turn chicken, season again and broil for another 10 minutes.

5. Serve warm and enjoy!

# Brie Stuffed Chicken Breasts

Preparation Time: 15 minutes
Cooking Time: 15 minutes
Servings: 3-4

## Recipe Ingredients:
- 2 (8-ounce) skinless, boneless chicken fillets
- Salt and ground black pepper, as required
- 4 brie cheese slices
- 1 tablespoon of fresh chive, minced
- 4 bacon slices

## Cooking Instruction:
1. Cut each chicken fillet in 2 equal-sized pieces, then carefully, make a slit in each chicken piece horizontally about ¼-inch from the edge.

2. Open each chicken piece and season with salt and black pepper. Place 1 cheese slice in the open area of each chicken piece and sprinkle with chives.

3. Close the chicken pieces and wrap each one with a bacon slice. Secure with toothpicks. Press AIR OVEN MODE button of Ninja Foodi Dual Heat Air Fry Oven and turn the dial to select "Air Fry" mode.

4. Press TIME/SLICES button and again turn the dial to set the cooking time to 15 minutes. Now push TEMP/SHADE button.

5. Rotate the dial to set the temperature at 355°F. Press "Start/Stop" button to start. When the unit beeps to signal that it is preheated.

6. Open the oven door and grease the air fry basket. Place the chicken pieces into the prepared air fry basket and insert in the oven.

7. When cooking time is completed, open the oven door and place the rolled chicken breasts onto a cutting board.

8. Cut into desired-sized slices and serve.

# Simple Turkey Breast

Preparation Time: 10 minutes
Cooking Time: 1 hour 20 minutes
Servings: 5-6

## Recipe Ingredients:
- 1 (2¾-pound) bone-in, skin-on turkey breast half
- Salt and ground black pepper, as required

## Cooking Instruction:
1. Rub the turkey breast with the salt and black pepper evenly. Arrange the turkey breast into a greased SearPlate.

2. Press AIR OVEN MODE button of Ninja Foodi Dual Heat Air Fry Oven and turn the dial to select "Bake" mode.

3. Press TIME/SLICES button and again turn the dial to set the cooking time to 1 hour 20 minutes.

4. Now, push TEMP/SHADE button and rotate the dial to set the temperature at 450°F. Press "Start/Stop" button to start.

5. When the unit beeps to show that it is preheated, open the oven door. Insert the SearPlate in the oven.

6. When cooking time is completed, open the oven door and place the turkey breast onto a cutting board.

7. With a piece of foil, cover the turkey breast for about 20 minutes before slicing. Then, with a sharp knife, cut the turkey breast into desired size slices and serve.

# Chicken Kabobs

Preparation Time: 15 minutes
Cooking Time: 9 minutes
Servings: 1-2

## Recipe Ingredients:

- 1 (8-ounce) chicken breast, cut into medium-sized pieces
- 1 tablespoon of fresh lemon juice
- 3 garlic cloves, grated
- 1 tablespoon of fresh oregano, minced
- ½ teaspoon of lemon zest, grated
- Salt and ground black pepper, as required
- 1 teaspoon of plain Greek yogurt
- 1 teaspoon of olive oil

## Cooking Instruction:

1. In a large bowl, add the chicken, lemon juice, garlic, oregano, lemon zest, salt and black pepper and toss to coat well.

2. Cover the bowl and refrigerate overnight. Remove the bowl from the refrigerator and stir in the yogurt and oil.

3. Thread the chicken pieces onto the metal skewers. Press AIR OVEN MODE button of Ninja Foodi Dual Heat Air Fry Oven and turn the dial to select "Air Fry" mode.

4. Press TIME/SLICES button and again turn the dial to set the cooking time to 9 minutes. Now push TEMP/SHADE button.

5. Rotate the dial to set the temperature at 350°F. Press "Start/Stop" button to start. When the unit beeps to show that it is preheated.

6. Open the oven door and grease the air fry basket. Place the skewers into the prepared air fry basket and insert in the oven.

7. Flip the skewers once halfway through. When cooking time is completed, open the oven door and serve hot.

# Oat Crusted Chicken Breasts

Preparation Time: 15 minutes
Cooking Time: 12 minutes
Servings: 1-2

## Recipe Ingredients:
- 2 (6-ounce) chicken breasts
- Salt and ground black pepper, as required
- ¾ cup of oats
- 2 tablespoons of mustard powder
- 1 tablespoon of fresh parsley
- 2 medium eggs

## Cooking Instruction:
1. Place the chicken breasts onto a cutting board and with a meat mallet, flatten each into even thickness. Then, cut each breast in half.

2. Sprinkle the chicken pieces with salt and black pepper and set aside. In a blender, add the oats, mustard powder, parsley, salt and black pepper.

3. Pulse until a coarse breadcrumb-like mixture is formed. Transfer the oat mixture into a shallow bowl. In another bowl, crack the eggs and beat well.

4. Coat the chicken with oats mixture and then, dip into beaten eggs and again, coat with the oat mixture.

5. Press AIR OVEN MODE button of Ninja Foodi Dual Heat Air Fry Oven and turn the dial to select "Air Fry" mode.

6. Press TIME/SLICES button and again turn the dial to set the cooking time to 12 minutes. Now push TEMP/SHADE button.

7. Rotate the dial to set the temperature at 350°F. Press "Start/Stop" button to start. When the unit beeps to show that it is preheated, open the oven door and grease the air fry basket.

8. Place the chicken breasts into the prepared air fry basket and insert in the oven. Flip the chicken breasts once halfway through.

9. When cooking time is completed, open the oven door and serve hot.

# Roasted Goose

**Preparation Time:** 15 minutes
**Cooking Time:** 40 minutes
**Servings:** 11-12

## Recipe Ingredients:
- 8 pounds of goose
- Juice of a lemon
- Salt and pepper
- ½ yellow onion, peeled and chopped
- 1 head garlic, peeled and chopped
- ½ cup of wine
- 1 teaspoon of dried thyme

## Cooking Instruction:
1. Place the goose in a SearPlate and whisk the rest of the ingredients in a bowl.

2. Pour this thick sauce over the goose and brush it liberally. Transfer the goose to Ninja Foodi Dual Heat Air Fry Oven and close the door.

3. Select "Air Roast" mode by rotating the dial. Press the TEMP/SHADE button and change the value to 355 °F.

4. Press the TIME/SLICES button and change the value to 40 minutes, then press Start/Stop to begin cooking.

5. Serve warm.

# Crispy Chicken Cutlets

Preparation Time: 15 minutes
Cooking Time: 30 minutes
Servings: 3-4

## Recipe Ingredients:
- ¾ cup flour
- 2 large eggs
- 1½ cups of breadcrumbs
- ¼ cup of Parmesan cheese, grated
- 1 tablespoon of mustard powder
- Salt and ground black pepper, as required
- 4 (6-ounce) (¼-inch thick) skinless, boneless chicken cutlets

## Cooking Instruction:
1. In a shallow bowl, add the flour. In a second bowl, crack the eggs and beat well.

2. In a third bowl, mix together the breadcrumbs, cheese, mustard powder, salt, and black pepper. Season the chicken with salt, and black pepper.

3. Coat the chicken with flour, then dip into beaten eggs and finally coat with the breadcrumbs mixture.

4. Press AIR OVEN MODE button of Ninja Foodi Dual Heat Air Fry Oven and turn the dial to select "Air Fry" mode.

5. Press TIME/SLICES button and again turn the dial to set the cooking time to 30 minutes. Now push TEMP/SHADE button.

6. Rotate the dial to set the temperature at 355°F. Press "Start/Stop" button to start. When the unit beeps to show that it is preheated.

7. Open the oven door and grease the air fry basket. Place the chicken cutlets into the prepared air fry basket and insert in the oven.

8. When cooking time is completed, open the oven door and serve hot.

# Blackened Chicken Bake

Preparation Time: 15 minutes
Cooking Time: 18 minutes
Servings: 3-4

## Recipe Ingredients:
- 4 chicken breasts
- 2 teaspoons of olive oil
- Chopped parsley, for garnish

## Seasoning:
- 1½ tablespoons of brown sugar
- 1 teaspoon of paprika
- 1 teaspoon of dried oregano
- ¼ teaspoon of garlic powder
- ½ teaspoon of salt and pepper

## Cooking Instruction:
1. Mix olive oil with brown sugar, paprika, oregano, garlic powder, salt, and black pepper in a bowl.

2. Place the chicken breasts in the SearPlate of Ninja Foodi Dual Heat Air Fry Oven.

3. Transfer the SearPlate to Ninja Foodi Dual Heat Air Fry Oven and close the door.

4. Select "Bake" mode by rotating the dial. Press the TIME/SLICES button and change the value to 18 minutes.

5. Press the TEMP/SHADE button and change the value to 425°F. Press Start/Stop to begin cooking.

6. Serve warm.

# Herbed Duck Breast

Preparation Time: 15 minutes
Cooking Time: 20 minutes
Servings: 1-2

## Recipe Ingredients:
- 1 (10-ounce) duck breast
- Olive oil cooking spray
- ½ tablespoon of fresh thyme, chopped
- ½ tablespoon of fresh rosemary, chopped
- 1 cup of chicken broth
- 1 tablespoon of fresh lemon juice
- Salt and ground black pepper, as required

## Cooking Instruction:
1. Spray the duck breast with cooking spray evenly. In a bowl, mix well the remaining ingredients.

2. Add the duck breast and coat with the marinade generously. Refrigerate, covered for about 4 hours. With a piece of foil, cover the duck breast.

3. Press AIR OVEN MODE button of Ninja Foodi Dual Heat Air Fry Oven and turn the dial to select "Air Fry" mode.

4. Press TIME/SLICES button and again turn the dial to set the cooking time to 15 minutes. Now push TEMP/SHADE button.

5. Rotate the dial to set the temperature at 390°F. Press "Start/Stop" button to start. When the unit beeps to show that it is preheated, open the oven door and grease the air fry basket.

6. Then, place the duck breast into the prepared air fry basket and insert in the oven. After 15 minutes of cooking, set the temperature to 355°F for 5 minutes.

7. When cooking time is completed, open the oven door and serve hot.

# Brine-Soaked Turkey

**Preparation Time:** 15 minutes
**Cooking Time:** 60 minutes
**Servings:** 3-4

## Recipe Ingredients:
- 7 pounds bone-in, skin-on turkey breast

**Brine**
- ½ cup of salt
- 1 lemon
- ½ onion
- 3 cloves garlic, smashed
- 5 sprigs fresh thyme
- 3 bay leaves
- black pepper

**Turkey Breast**
- 4 tablespoons of butter, softened
- ½ teaspoon of black pepper
- ½ teaspoon of garlic powder
- ¼ teaspoon of dried thyme
- ¼ teaspoon of dried oregano

## Cooking Instruction:
1. Mix the turkey brine ingredients in a pot and soak the turkey in the brine overnight. The next day, remove the soaked turkey from the brine.

2. Whisk the butter, black pepper, garlic powder, oregano, and thyme. Brush the butter mixture over the turkey, then place it in a SearPlate.

3. Transfer the SearPlate to Ninja Foodi Dual Heat Air Fry Oven and close the door. Select "Air Roast" mode by rotating the dial.

4. Press the TIME/SLICES button and change the value to 60 minutes. Press the TEMP/SHADE button and change the value to 375°F.

5. Press Start/Stop to begin cooking.

6. Slice and serve warm.

# Chicken Kebabs

Preparation Time: 15 minutes
Cooking Time: 20 minutes
Servings: 5-6

## Recipe Ingredients:
- 16 ounces skinless chicken breasts, cubed
- 2 tablespoons of soy sauce
- ½ zucchini sliced
- 1 tablespoon of chicken seasoning
- 1 teaspoon of BBQ seasoning
- salt and pepper to taste
- ½ green pepper sliced
- ½ red pepper sliced
- ½ yellow pepper sliced   ¼ red onion sliced
- 4 cherry tomatoes
- cooking spray

## Cooking Instruction:
1. At first, toss chicken and veggies with all the spices and seasoning in a bowl. Alternatively, thread them on skewers and place these skewers in the air fry basket.

2. Transfer the basket to Ninja Foodi Dual Heat Air Fry Oven and close the door. Select "Air Fry" mode by rotating the dial.

3. Press the TIME/SLICES button and change the value to 20 minutes. Press the TEMP/SHADE button and change the value to 350°F.

4. Press Start/Stop to begin cooking. Flip the skewers when cooked halfway through, then resume cooking.

5. Serve warm.

# Roasted Duck

Preparation Time: 15 minutes
Cooking Time: 3 hours
Servings: 5-6

## Recipe Ingredients:
- 6 pounds of whole Pekin duck
- Salt, to taste
- 5 garlic cloves, chopped
- 1 lemon, chopped

## Glaze
- ½ cup balsamic vinegar
- 1 lemon, juiced
- ¼ cup honey

## Cooking Instruction:

1. Place the Pekin duck in a baking tray and add garlic, lemon, and salt on top. Whisk honey, the juiced lemon, and vinegar in a bowl.

2. Brush this glaze over the duck liberally. Marinate overnight in the refrigerator. Remove the duck from the marinade and move the duck to SearPlate.

3. Transfer the SearPlate to Ninja Foodi Dual Heat Air Fry Oven and close the door. Select "Air Roast" mode by rotating the dial.

4. Press the TIME/SLICES button and change the value to 2 hours. Press the TEMP/SHADE button and change the value to 350°F.

5. Press Start/Stop to begin cooking. When cooking completed, set the oven the temperature to 350°F and time to 1 hour at Air Roast mode.

6. Press Start/Stop to begin. When it is cooked, serve warm.

# Parmesan Chicken Meatballs

Preparation Time: 15 minutes
Cooking Time: 12 minutes
Servings: 3-4

## Recipe Ingredients:
- 1 pound of ground chicken
- 1 large egg, beaten
- ½ cup of Parmesan cheese, grated
- ½ cup of pork rinds, ground
- 1 teaspoon of garlic powder
- 1 teaspoon of paprika
- 1 teaspoon of kosher salt
- ½ teaspoon of pepper
- ½ cup of ground pork rinds, for crust

## Cooking Instruction:
1. Toss all the meatball ingredients in a bowl and mix well. Make small meatballs out of this mixture and roll them in the pork rinds.

2. Place the coated meatballs in the air fry basket. Transfer the basket to Ninja Foodi Dual Heat Air Fry Oven and close the door.

3. Select "Bake" mode by rotating the dial. Press the TIME/SLICES button and change the value to 12 minutes.

4. Press the TEMP/SHADE button and change the value to 400°F. Press Start/Stop to begin cooking.

5. Once preheated, place the air fry basket inside and close its oven door.

6. Serve warm.

# Chicken and Rice Casserole

Preparation Time: 15 minutes
Cooking Time: 23 minutes
Servings: 3-4

## Recipe Ingredients:
- 2 pounds of bone-in chicken thighs
- Salt and black pepper
- 1 teaspoon of olive oil
- 5 cloves garlic, chopped
- 2 large onions, chopped
- 2 large red bell peppers, chopped
- 1 tablespoon of sweet Hungarian paprika
- 1 teaspoon of hot Hungarian paprika
- 2 tablespoons of tomato paste
- 2 cups of chicken broth
- 3 cups of brown rice, thawed
- 2 tablespoons of parsley, chopped
- 6 tablespoons of sour cream

## Cooking Instruction:
1. Season the chicken with salt, black pepper, and olive oil. Sear the chicken in a skillet for 5 minutes per side, then transfer to SearPlate.

2. Sauté onion in the same skillet until soft. Toss in garlic, peppers, and paprika, then sauté for 3 minutes.

3. Stir in tomato paste, chicken broth, and rice. Mix well and cook until rice is soft, then add sour cream and parsley.

4. Spread the mixture over the chicken in the SearPlate. Transfer the SearPlate to Ninja Foodi Dual Heat Air Fry Oven and close the door.

5. Transfer the sandwich to Ninja Foodi Dual Heat Air Fry Oven and close the door. Select "Bake" mode by rotating the dial.

6. Press the TIME/SLICES button and change the value to 10 minutes. Press the TEMP/SHADE button and change the value to 375°F.

7. Press Start/Stop to begin cooking.

8. Serve warm.

# Chicken Potato Bake

Preparation Time: 15 minutes
Cooking Time: 25 minutes
Servings: 3-4

## Recipe Ingredients:
- 4 potatoes, diced
- 1 tablespoon of garlic, minced
- 1.5 tablespoons of olive oil
- ⅛ teaspoon of salt
- ⅛ teaspoon of pepper
- 1.5 pounds of boneless skinless chicken
- ¾ cup of mozzarella cheese, shredded
- Parsley, chopped

## Cooking Instruction:
1. Toss chicken and potatoes with all the spices and oil in a SearPlate. Drizzle the cheese on top of the chicken and potato.

2. Transfer the SearPlate to Ninja Foodi Dual Heat Air Fry Oven and close the door. Select "Bake" mode by rotating the dial.

3. Press the TIME/SLICES button and change the value to 25 minutes. Press the TEMP/SHADE button and change the value to 375°F.

4. Press Start/Stop to begin cooking.

5. Serve warm.

# Spanish Chicken Bake

**Preparation Time:** 15 minutes
**Cooking Time:** 25 minutes
**Servings:** 3-4

## Recipe Ingredients:
- ½ onion, quartered
- ½ red onion, quartered
- ½ pound of potatoes, quartered
- 4 garlic cloves
- 4 tomatoes, quartered
- ⅛ cup of chorizo
- ¼ teaspoon of paprika powder
- 4 chicken thighs, boneless
- ¼ teaspoon of dried oregano
- ½ green bell pepper, julienned
- Salt, to taste
- Black pepper, to taste

## Cooking Instruction:
1. Toss chicken, veggies, and all the ingredients in a SearPlate. Transfer the SearPlate into Ninja Foodi Dual Heat Air Fry Oven and close the door.

2. Select "Bake" mode by rotating the dial. Press the TIME/SLICES button and change the value to 25 minutes.

3. Press the TEMP/SHADE button and change the value to 425°F. Press Start/Stop to begin cooking.

4. Serve warm.

# Chapter 6: Red Meat Recipes

## Beef Short Ribs

Preparation Time: 15 minutes
Cooking Time: 35 minutes
Servings: 3-4

### Recipe Ingredients:
- 1⅔ pounds of short ribs
- Salt and black pepper, to taste
- 1 teaspoon of grated garlic
- ½ teaspoon of salt
- 1 teaspoon of cumin seeds
- ¼ cup of panko crumbs
- 1 teaspoon of ground cumin
- 1 teaspoon of avocado oil
- ½ teaspoon of orange zest
- 1 egg, beaten

### Cooking Instruction:
1. At first, place the beef ribs in a SearPlate and pour the whisked egg on top. Whisk the rest of the crusting ingredients in a bowl and spread over the beef.

2. Transfer the SearPlate to Ninja Foodi Dual Heat Air Fry Oven and close the door. Select "Air Fry" mode by rotating the dial.

3. Press the TIME/SLICES button and change the value to 35 minutes. Press the TEMP/SHADE button and change the value to 350°F.

4. Press Start/Stop to begin cooking.

5. Serve warm.

# Savory Pork Roast

Preparation Time: 10 minutes
Cooking Time: 1 hour
Servings: 2-3

## Recipe Ingredients:
- ¼ teaspoon of dried thyme
- 1 tablespoon of fresh rosemary, divided
- 1 teaspoon of garlic salt
- ⅛ teaspoon of black pepper, freshly ground
- 1½ pounds of pork loin roast, boneless

## Cooking Instruction:
1. Turn on your Ninja Foodi Dual Heat Air Fry Oven and rotate the knob to select "Air Roast".

2. Preheat by selecting the timer for 3 minutes and temperature for 350°F. Take a bowl mix well rosemary, garlic salt, thyme, and pepper together.

3. Now add pork to coat well. Take a dish and place coated pork on it. Roast pork for about an hour in preheated Ninja Foodi Dual Heat Air Fry Oven at 350°F.

4. Serve and enjoy!

# Czech Roast Pork

Preparation Time: 20 minutes
Cooking Time: 3 hours 30 minutes
Servings: 3-4

## Recipe Ingredients:
- 1 tablespoon of caraway seeds
- ½ tablespoon of garlic powder
- 1 tablespoon of vegetable oil
- ½ tablespoon of prepared mustard
- ½ tablespoon of salt
- 1½ medium onions, chopped
- 2 pounds of pork shoulder blade roast
- 1 teaspoon of ground black pepper
- ¼ cup of beer

## Cooking Instruction:
1. Take a bowl and add garlic powder, mustard, vegetable oil, caraway seeds, salt and pepper to form a paste.

2. Then rub the paste over pork roast and let it sit for about 30 minutes. Turn on your Ninja Foodi Dual Heat Air Fry Oven.

3. Rotate the knob to select "Air Roast". Preheat by selecting the timer for 3 minutes and temperature for 350°F. Take a SearPlate and add onions.

4. Pour in the beer and place pork. Cover it with a foil. Roast for about an hour in preheated Ninja Foodi Dual Heat Air Fry Oven at 350°F.

5. Remove foil, turn roast and let it roast for 2 hours and 30 minutes more. Remove from oven and set aside for 10 minutes before slicing.

6. Serve warm and enjoy!

# Herby Pork Bake

Preparation Time: 10 minutes
Cooking Time: 40 minutes
Servings: 1-2

## Recipe Ingredients:
- 1 pork loin steak, cut into bite-sized pieces
- ½ red onion, cut into wedges
- 1 potato, halved
- ½ carrot, halved
- ½ tablespoon of olive oil
- 1 tablespoon of mixed dried herbs
- 4 tablespoons of Cider Pour Over Sauce

## Cooking Instruction:
1. Turn on your Ninja Foodi Dual Heat Air Fry Oven and rotate the knob to select "Bake".

2. Next, preheat by selecting the timer for 3 minutes and temperature for 420°F. Take the SearPlate and toss pork, onion, potatoes and carrots with herbs and olive oil.

3. Bake for about 25 minutes in preheated Ninja Foodi Dual Heat Air Fry Oven at 420°F. Remove from the oven and add sauce on top.

4. Bake for 5 more minutes so that you have a bubbling sauce.

5. Serve and enjoy!

# Roasted Pork Belly

Preparation Time: 10 minutes
Cooking Time: 1 hour 30 minutes
Servings: 7-8

## Recipe Ingredients:
- ¾ teaspoon of dried oregano
- ¾ teaspoon of ground cumin
- ¾ teaspoon of ground black pepper
- ¾ teaspoon of salt
- ¾ teaspoon of paprika
- ¾ teaspoon of onion powder
- ¾ teaspoon of ground turmeric
- ¾ teaspoon of garlic powder
- 2 pounds of whole pork belly
- Cayenne pepper, to taste
- 1 tablespoon of lemon juice

## Cooking Instruction:
1. Take a bowl and add garlic powder, onion powder, turmeric, cayenne pepper, paprika, oregano, cumin, salt and pepper.

2. Rub the mixture onto pork belly. Cover with a plastic wrap and refrigerate for at least 2 hours.

3. Turn on your Ninja Foodi Dual Heat Air Fry Oven and rotate the knob to select "Air Roast".

4. Preheat by selecting the timer for 3 minutes and temperature for 450°F. Line a SearPlate with parchment paper.

5. Place pork belly onto the prepared dish, with shallow cuts. Rub lemon juice on top.

6. Roast for about 40 minutes in preheated Ninja Foodi Dual Heat Air Fry Oven at 350°F until fat is crispy.

7. Remove from oven and set aside for 10 minutes before slicing.

8. Serve warm and enjoy!

# Baked Beef Stew

Preparation Time: 15 minutes
Cooking Time: 2 hours
Servings: 3-4

## Recipe Ingredients:

- 1 pound of beef-stew, cut into cubes
- ½ cup of water
- 2 tablespoons of instant tapioca
- ½ can dried tomatoes with juice
- 1 teaspoon of white sugar
- ½ tablespoon of beef bouillon granules
- ¾ teaspoon of salt
- ⅛ teaspoon of ground black pepper
- 1 strip celery, cut into ¾ inch pieces
- ½ onion, chopped
- 2 carrots, cut into 1-inch pieces
- ½ slice bread, cubed
- 2 potatoes, peeled and cubed

## Cooking Instruction:

1. Turn on your Ninja Foodi Dual Heat Air Fry Oven and rotate the knob to select "Bake".

2. Preheat by selecting the timer for 2 hours and temperature for 375°F. Grease a SearPlate. Take a large pan over medium heat and brown the stew meat.

3. Meanwhile, take a bowl and mix together tomatoes, water, tapioca, beef bouillon granules, sugar, salt and pepper.

4. Add prepared brown beef, celery, potatoes, carrots, onion and bread cubes. Pour in the greased SearPlate.

5. Bake for about 2 hours in preheated Ninja Foodi Dual Heat Air Fry Oven at 375°F.

6. Remove from oven and set aside for 2 minutes.

7. Serve warm and enjoy!

# Russian Baked Beef

Preparation Time: 10 minutes
Cooking Time: 1 hour
Servings: 2-3

## Recipe Ingredients:
- ½ beef tenderloin
- 1 onion, sliced
- ¾ cup of Cheddar cheese, grated
- ½ cup of milk
- 1½ tablespoons of mayonnaise
- Salt and black pepper, to taste

## Cooking Instruction:
1. Turn on your Ninja Foodi Dual Heat Air Fry Oven and rotate the knob to select "Bake".

2. Preheat by selecting the timer for 60 minutes and temperature for 350°F. Grease a SearPlate.

3. Cut the beef into thick slices and place in the SearPlate. Season beef with salt and pepper and cover with onion slices. Also, spread cheese on top.

4. Then, take a separate bowl and stir together milk and mayonnaise and pour over cheese.

5. Bake for about an hour in preheated Ninja Foodi Dual Heat Air Fry Oven at 350°F.

6. Remove from oven and set aside for 2 minutes.

7. Serve warm and enjoy!

# Lamb Chops

Preparation Time: 5 minutes
Cooking Time: 15 minutes
Servings: 3-4

## Recipe Ingredients:
- 4 medium lamb chops
- 2 tablespoons of olive oil
- 1 garlic clove, crushed
- 3 thin lemon slices
- ½ teaspoon of dried oregano
- ¼ teaspoon of black pepper, freshly ground
- ½ teaspoon of kosher salt

## Cooking Instruction:

1. Take a dish and mix together salt, pepper, olive oil, lemon slices, garlic, and oregano. Then, add lamb in the dish and marinate for about 4 hours.

2. Turn on your Ninja Foodi Dual Heat Air Fry Oven and rotate the knob to select "Bake".

3. Preheat by selecting the timer for 8 to 10 minutes and temperature for 400°F.

4. Meanwhile, take a pan and add oil and heat over medium heat and cook each side of pork for 3 minutes until brown.

5. Bake for about 8 to 10 minutes in preheated Ninja Foodi Dual Heat Air Fry Oven at 400°F.

6. Remove from oven and set aside for 2 minutes.

7. Serve warm and enjoy!

# Lamb and Potato Bake

Preparation Time: 8 minutes
Cooking Time: 55 minutes
Servings: 1-2

## Recipe Ingredients:
- 2 potatoes
- ¾ lean lamb mince
- ½ teaspoon of cinnamon
- ½ tablespoon of olive oil
- 4 cups of tomato pasta sauce
- 1 cup of cheese sauce

## Cooking Instruction:
1. At first, boil the potatoes for 12 minutes or until half cooked. Meanwhile, take a pan and heat oil over medium heat.

2. Add lamb mince into brown. Use a spoon to break up lumps. Add cinnamon and fry for about a minute.

3. Pour in the tomato sauce and leave for about 5 minutes. Once the potatoes are done, thinly slice them.

4. Turn on your Ninja Foodi Dual Heat Air Fry Oven and rotate the knob to select "Bake".

5. Select the timer for 35 minutes and temperature for 390°F. Place everything on a SearPlate and spread cheeses on top.

6. Bake until well cooked.

7. Serve and enjoy!

# Ground Beef Casserole

Preparation Time: 8 minutes
Cooking Time: 25 minutes
Servings: 2-3

## Recipe Ingredients:

- ¼ medium onion, chopped
- ½ pound of extra lean ground beef
- ½ pound of penne
- ½ tablespoon of olive oil
- ½ clove garlic, minced
- ½ cup of marinara sauce
- 1 cup of cheddar cheese, shredded
- Salt and pepper to taste

## Cooking Instruction:

1. Take a large pot with lightly salted water and bring it to a boil. Add penne and let it cook for about 10 minutes.

2. Take a pan and add oil, beef and onion. Fry for about 10 minutes over medium-high heat and add garlic.

3. Stir in the marinara sauce and add salt and pepper according to taste, then drain the pasta and pour into the SearPlate.

4. Add the beef-marinara mixture on top of the penne pasta. Lastly, add cheese with cheese.

5. Turn on your Ninja Foodi Dual Heat Air Fry Oven and rotate the knob to select "Bake".

6. Select the timer for 10 minutes and temperature for 400°F. Press Star/Stop button to begin preheating.

7. Bake for about 10 minutes in preheated Ninja Foodi Dual Heat Air Fry Oven until the cheese is nicely melted.

8. Serve immediately.

# Tarragon Beef Shanks

Preparation Time: **15** minutes
Cooking Time: 15 minutes
Servings: 3-4

## Recipe Ingredients:
- 2 tablespoons of olive oil
- 2 pounds of beef shank
- Salt and black pepper to taste
- 1 onion, diced
- 2 stalks celery, diced
- 1 cup of Marsala wine
- 2 tablespoons of dried tarragon

## Cooking Instruction:
1. Place the beef shanks in a baking pan. Whisk the rest of the ingredients in a bowl and pour over the shanks. Place these shanks in the air fry basket.

2. Transfer the basket to Ninja Foodi Dual Heat Air Fry Oven and close the door. Select "Air Fry" mode by rotating the dial.

3. Press the TIME/SLICES button and change the value to 15 minutes. Press the TEMP/SHADE button and change the value to 375°F.

4. Press Start/Stop to begin cooking.

5. Serve warm and enjoy!

# Garlic Braised Ribs

Preparation Time: 15 minutes
Cooking Time: 20 minutes
Servings: 7-8

## Recipe Ingredients:
- 2 tablespoons of vegetable oil
- 5 pounds of bone-in short ribs
- Salt and black pepper, to taste
- 2 heads garlic, halved
- 1 medium onion, chopped
- 4 ribs celery, chopped
- 2 medium carrots, chopped
- 3 tablespoons of tomato paste
- ¼ cup of dry red wine
- ¼ cup of beef stock
- 4 sprigs thyme
- 1 cup of parsley, chopped
- ½ cup of chives, chopped
- 1 tablespoon of lemon zest, grated

## Cooking Instruction:
1. Toss everything in a large bowl, then add short ribs. Mix well to soak the ribs and marinate for 30 minutes.

2. Next, transfer the soaked ribs to the SearPlate and add the marinade around them. Transfer the SearPlate to Ninja Foodi Dual Heat Air Fry Oven and close the door.

3. Select "Air Fry" mode by rotating the dial. Press the TIME/SLICES button and change the value to 20 minutes.

4. Press the TEMP/SHADE button and change the value to 400°F. Press Start/Stop to begin cooking.

5. Serve warm.

# Beef Zucchini Shashliks

Preparation Time: 15 minutes
Cooking Time: 25 minutes
Servings: 3-4

## Recipe Ingredients:
- 1 pound of beef, boned and diced
- 1 lime, juiced, and chopped
- 3 tablespoons of olive oil
- 20 garlic cloves, chopped
- 1 handful rosemary, chopped
- 3 green peppers, cubed
- 2 zucchinis, cubed
- 2 red onions, cut into wedges

## Cooking Instruction:
1. Toss the beef with the rest of the skewer's ingredients in a bowl. Thread the beef, peppers, zucchini, and onion on the skewers.

2. Place these beef skewers in the air fry basket. Transfer the basket to Ninja Foodi Dual Heat Air Fry Oven and close the door.

3. Select "Air Fry" mode by rotating the dial. Press the TIME/SLICES button and change the value to 25 minutes.

4. Press the TEMP/SHADE button and change the value to 370°F. Press Start/Stop to begin cooking.

5. Flip the skewers when cooked halfway through, then resume cooking.

6. Serve warm.

# Mint Lamb with Toasted Hazelnuts

**Preparation Time:** 15 minutes
**Cooking Time:** 25 minutes
**Servings:** 3-4

## Recipe Ingredients:
- ¼ cup of hazelnuts, toasted
- ⅔ pound of shoulder lamb, cut into strips
- 1 tablespoon of hazelnut oil
- 2 tablespoons of mint leaves, chopped
- ½ cup of frozen peas
- ¼ cup of water
- ½ cup of white wine
- Salt and black pepper to taste

## Cooking Instruction:
1. At first, toss lamb with hazelnuts, spices, and all the ingredients in a SearPlate.

2. Transfer the SearPlate to Ninja Foodi Dual Heat Air Fry Oven and close the door.

3. Select "Bake" mode by rotating the dial. Press the TIME/SLICES button and change the value to 25 minutes.

4. Press the TEMP/SHADE button and change the value to 370°F. Press Start/Stop to begin cooking.

5. Serve warm.

# Lamb Chops with Rosemary Sauce

Preparation Time: 15 minutes
Cooking Time: 45 minutes
Servings: 7-8

## Recipe Ingredients:
- 8 lamb loin chops
- 1 small onion, peeled and chopped
- Salt and black pepper, to taste

**For the sauce:**
- 1 onion, peeled and chopped
- 1 tablespoon of rosemary leaves
- 1 ounce of butter
- 1 ounce of plain flour
- 6 ounces of milk
- 6 ounces of vegetable stock
- 2 tablespoons of cream, whipping
- Salt and black pepper, to taste

## Cooking Instruction:
1. At first, place the lamb loin chops and onion in a SearPlate, then drizzle salt and black pepper on top.

2. Transfer the SearPlate to Ninja Foodi Dual Heat Air Fry Oven and close the door. Select "Air Fry" mode by rotating the dial.

3. Press the TIME/SLICES button and change the value to 45 minutes. Press the TEMP/SHADE button and change the value to 350°F.

4. Press Start/Stop to begin cooking. Prepare the white sauce by melting butter in a suitable saucepan, then stir in onions.

5. Sauté for 5 minutes, stir in flour and stir cook for 2 minutes. Stir in the rest of the ingredients and allow to mix well.

6. Pour the sauce over baked chops and serve.

# Garlicky Lamb Chops

Preparation Time: 15 minutes
Cooking Time: 45 minutes
Servings: 7-8

## Recipe Ingredients:
- 8 medium lamb chops
- ¼ cup of olive oil
- 3 thin lemon slices
- 2 garlic cloves, crushed
- 1 teaspoon of dried oregano
- 1 teaspoon of salt
- ½ teaspoon of black pepper

## Cooking Instruction:
1. At first, place the medium lamb chops in a SearPlate and rub them with olive oil. Add lemon slices, garlic, oregano, salt, and black pepper on top of the lamb chops.

2. Transfer the SearPlate to Ninja Foodi Dual Heat Air Fry Oven and close the door. Select "Air Roast" mode by rotating the dial.

3. Press the TIME/SLICES button and change the value to 45 minutes. Press the TEMP/SHADE button and change the value to 400°F.

4. Press Start/Stop to begin cooking.

5. Serve warm.

# Lamb Kebabs

Preparation Time: 15 minutes
Cooking Time: 20 minutes
Servings: 3-4

## Recipe Ingredients:
- 18 ounces lamb mince
- 1 teaspoon of chili powder
- 1 teaspoon of cumin powder
- 1 egg
- 2 ounces of onion, chopped
- 2 teaspoons of sesame oil

## Cooking Instruction:
1. Whisk onion with egg, chili powder, oil, cumin powder, and salt in a bowl. Add lamb to coat well, then thread it on the skewers.

2. Place these lamb skewers in the air fry basket. Transfer the basket to Ninja Foodi Dual Heat Air Fry Oven and close the door.

3. Select "Air Fry" mode by rotating the dial. Press the TIME/SLICES button and change the value to 20 minutes.

4. Press the TEMP/SHADE button and change the value to 395°F. Press Start/Stop to begin cooking.

5. Serve warm.

# Lamb Rack with Lemon Crust

Preparation Time: 15 minutes
Cooking Time: 25 minutes
Servings: 2-3

## Recipe Ingredients:
- 1 ⅔ pounds of Frenched rack of lamb
- Salt and black pepper, to taste
- ¼ pound of dry breadcrumbs
- 1 teaspoon of garlic, grated
- ½ teaspoon of salt
- 1 teaspoon of cumin seeds
- 1 teaspoon of ground cumin
- 1 teaspoon of oil
- ½ teaspoon of grated lemon rind
- 1 egg, beaten

## Cooking Instruction:

1. At first, place the lamb rack in a SearPlate and pour the whisked egg on top. Whisk the rest of the crusting ingredients in a bowl and spread over the lamb.

2. Transfer the SearPlate to Ninja Foodi Dual Heat Air Fry Oven and close the door. Select "Air Fry" mode by rotating the dial.

3. Press the TIME/SLICES button and change the value to 25 minutes. Press the TEMP/SHADE button and change the value to 350°F.

4. Press Start/Stop to begin cooking.

5. Serve warm.

# Greek lamb Farfalle

Preparation Time: 15 minutes
Cooking Time: 20 minutes
Servings: 5-6

## Recipe Ingredients:
- 1 tablespoon of olive oil
- 1 onion, chopped
- 2 garlic cloves, chopped
- 2 teaspoons of dried oregano
- 1 pound of pack lamb mince
- ¾ pound of tin tomatoes, chopped
- ¼ cup of black olives pitted
- ½ cup of frozen spinach, defrosted
- 2 tablespoons of dill, removed and chopped
- 9 ounces farfalle paste, boiled
- 1 ball half-fat mozzarella, torn

## Cooking Instruction:

1. At first, sauté onion and garlic with oil in a pan over moderate heat for 5 minutes. Stir in tomatoes, spinach, dill, oregano, lamb, and olives.

2. Stir cook for 5 minutes. Next, spread the lamb in the SearPlate and carefully toss in the boiled Farfalle pasta.

3. Top the pasta lamb mix with mozzarella cheese, and rantsfer the SearPlate into Ninja Foodi Dual Heat Air Fry Oven and close the door.

4. Select "Air Fry" mode by rotating the dial. Press the TIME/SLICES button and change the value to 10 minutes.

5. Press the TEMP/SHADE button and change the value to 350°F. Press Start/Stop to begin cooking.

6. Serve warm.

# New York Strip Steak

Preparation Time: 5 minutes
Cooking Time: 8 minutes
Servings: 1-2

## Recipe Ingredients:
- ½ teaspoon of olive oil
- ½ New York strip steak
- Kosher salt and ground black pepper, to taste

## Cooking Instruction:
1. Coat the steak with oil and then, generously season with salt and black pepper. Once done, grease an air fry basket.

2. Place steak into the prepared air fry basket. Turn on your Ninja Foodi Dual Heat Air Fry Oven and rotate the knob to select "Air Fry".

3. Now, select the timer for about 7 to 8 minutes and temperature for 400°F. Remove from the oven.

4. Place the steak onto a cutting board for about 10 minutes before slicing. Cut the steak into desired-size slices and transfer onto serving plates.

5. Serve immediately.

# Minced Lamb Casserole

Preparation Time: 15 minutes
Cooking Time: 31 minutes
Servings: 5-6

## Recipe Ingredients:
- 2 tablespoons of olive oil
- 1 medium onion, chopped
- ½ pound of ground lamb
- 4 fresh mushrooms, sliced
- 1 cup of small pasta shells, cooked
- 2 cups of bottled marinara sauce
- 1 teaspoon of butter
- 4 teaspoons of flour
- 1 cup of milk
- 1 egg, beaten
- 1 cup of cheddar cheese, grated

## Cooking Instruction:
1. Firstly, put a wok on moderate heat and add oil to heat. Toss in onion and sauté until soft. Stir in mushrooms and lamb, then cook until meat is brown.

2. Add marinara sauce and cook it to a simmer. Stir in pasta, then spread this mixture in the SearPlate.

3. Now, prepare the sauce by melting butter in a suitable saucepan over moderate heat. Stir in flour and whisk well, pour in the milk.

4. Mix thoroughly and whisk ¼ cup of sauce with egg, then return it to the saucepan. Stir, cook for 1 minute, then pour this sauce over the lamb.

5. Drizzle cheese over the lamb casserole. Transfer the SearPlate to Ninja Foodi Dual Heat Air Fry Oven and close the door. Select "Bake" mode by rotating the dial.

6. Press the TIME/SLICES button and change the value to 30 minutes. Press the TEMP/SHADE button and change the value to 350°F.

7. Press Start/Stop to begin cooking.

8. Serve warm.

# Za'atar Chops

Preparation Time: 15 minutes
Cooking Time: 20 minutes
Servings: 7-8

## Recipe Ingredients:
- 8 pork loin chops, bone-in
- 1 tablespoon of Za'atar
- 3 garlic cloves, crushed
- 1 teaspoon of avocado oil
- 2 tablespoons of lemon juice
- 1¼ teaspoons of salt
- Black pepper, to taste

## Cooking Instruction:
1. Rub the pork chops with oil, za'atar, salt, lemon juice, garlic, and black pepper.

2. Place these chops in the air fry basket, then transfer the basket to Ninja Foodi Dual Heat Air Fry Oven and close the door.

3. Select "Air Fry" mode by rotating the dial. Press the TIME/SLICES button and change the value to 20 minutes.

4. Press the TEMP/SHADE button and change the value to 400°F. Press Start/Stop to begin cooking.

5. Flip the chops when cooked halfway through, then resume cooking.

6. Serve warm.

# Pork Chops with Cashew Sauce

**Preparation Time:** 15 minutes
**Cooking Time:** 52 minutes
**Servings:** 7-8

## Recipe Ingredients:
- 8 pork loin chops
- 1 small onion, peeled and chopped
- Salt and black pepper, to taste

**For the Sauce:**
- ¼ cup cashews, finely chopped
- 1 cup of cashew butter
- 1 ounce of wheat flour
- 6 fl. ounce of milk
- 6 fl. ounce of beef stock
- 2 tablespoons of coconut cream, whipping
- Salt and black pepper, to taste

## Cooking Instruction:

1. Place the pork loin chops and onion in the SearPlate, then drizzle salt and black pepper on top.

2. Next, transfer the SearPlate to Ninja Foodi Dual Heat Air Fry Oven and close the door. Select "Bake" mode by rotating the dial.

3. Press the TIME/SLICES button and change the value to 45 minutes. Press the TEMP/SHADE button and change the value to 375°F.

4. Press Start/Stop to begin cooking. Prepare the white sauce by first melting butter in a suitable saucepan, then stir in cashews.

5. Sauté for 5 minutes, then stir flour and stir cook for 2 minutes. Stir in the rest of the sauce ingredients and mix well.

6. Pour the sauce over baked chops and serve.

# American Roast Beef

**Preparation Time:** 5 minutes
**Cooking Time:** 1 hour
**Servings:** 2-3

## Recipe Ingredients:
- 1½ pounds of beef eye of round roast
- ¼ teaspoon of kosher salt
- ⅛ teaspoon of black pepper, freshly ground
- ¼ teaspoon of garlic powder

## Cooking Instruction:
1. Turn on your Ninja Foodi Dual Heat Air Fry Oven and rotate the knob to select "Air Roast".

2. Then, preheat by selecting the timer for 3 minutes and temperature for 375°F.

3. Place beef in a SearPlate and season with salt, garlic powder and pepper. Roast in oven for about an hour.

4. Remove from oven and set aside for 10 minutes before slicing.

5. Serve warm and enjoy!

# Roast Beef and Yorkshire Pudding

Preparation Time: 20 minutes
Cooking Time: 1 hour 50 minutes
Servings: 2-3

## Recipe Ingredients:
- 1 egg, beaten
- ½ cup of milk
- ½ cup of flour
- 1/8 teaspoon of salt
- Salt, to taste
- Freshly ground pepper, to taste
- 1 pound of rump roast
- Garlic powder, to taste

## Cooking Instruction:
1. At first, turn on your Ninja Foodi Dual Heat Air Fry Oven and rotate the knob to select "Air Roast". Set the timer for 90 minutes and temperature for 375°F.

2. When the unit beeps to signify it has preheated, place beef in a SearPlate and season with salt, garlic powder and pepper.

3. Roast in oven for about 90 minutes until the thickest part of the beef is at 135°F. Remove from oven, reserving drippings.

4. Take a small bowl, beat egg until foamy. Take a separate bowl, then stir salt and flour. Pour in the beaten egg and add milk.

5. Now, preheat by selecting the timer for 3 minutes and temperature for 400°F. Pour the reserved drippings to a tin.

6. Place in the preheated oven for about 3 minutes. Remove from oven, add the flour mixture into the hot drippings.

7. Return to oven and set the timer for 20 minutes or until brown.

8. Serve warm and enjoy!

# Baked Pork Chops

Preparation Time: 5 minutes
Cooking Time: 20 minutes
Servings: 1-2

## Recipe Ingredients:
- 2 boneless pork chops
- ½ tablespoon of olive oil
- ¾ tablespoon of brown sugar
- ½ teaspoon of onion powder
- 1 teaspoon of paprika
- ½ teaspoon of dried thyme
- ¼ teaspoon of black pepper
- ½ teaspoon of salt

## Cooking Instruction:
1. Turn on your Ninja Foodi Dual Heat Air Fry Oven and rotate the knob to select "Bake".

2. Next, preheat by selecting the timer for 3 minutes and temperature for 425°F. Take a dish and line SearPlate with parchment paper.

3. Arrange the pork chops on the prepared SearPlate. Take a small bowl and combine the brown sugar, onion powder, dried thyme, salt, pepper and paprika.

4. Rub the prepared mixture over pork chops evenly. Bake the pork chops in the preheated Ninja Foodi Dual Heat Air Fry Oven for 20 minutes at 425°F.

5. Once done, set them aside for 5 minutes and then serve.

# Chapter 7: Dessert Recipes

## Caramel Apple Pie

Preparation Time: 15 minutes
Cooking Time: 48 minutes
Servings: 5-6

### Recipe Ingredients:
**Topping**
- ¼ cup of all-purpose flour
- ⅓ cup of packed brown sugar
- 2 tablespoons of butter, softened
- ½ teaspoon of ground cinnamon

**Pie**
- 6 cups of sliced peeled tart apples
- 1 tablespoon of lemon juice
- ½ cup of sugar
- 3 tablespoons of all-purpose flour
- ½ teaspoon of ground cinnamon
- 1 unbaked pastry shell (9 inches)
- 28 caramels
- 1 can (5 ounces) evaporated milk

### Cooking Instruction:
1. Mix flour with cinnamon, butter, and brown sugar. Spread this mixture in the SearPlate.

2. Next, transfer the SearPlate to Ninja Foodi Dual Heat Air Fry Oven and close the door. Select "Bake" mode by rotating the dial.

3. Press the TIME/SLICES button and change the value to 8 minutes. Press the TEMP/SHADE button and change the value to 350°F.

4. Press Start/Stop to begin cooking. Meanwhile, mix apple with lemon juice, cinnamon, flour, and sugar. Spread the filling in the baked crust.

5. Return to the air fryer oven. Bake again for 35 minutes in the oven, then mix caramels with milk in a pan and cook until melted.

6. Spread the caramel on top of the pie and bake for 5 minutes.

7. Serve.

# Peanut Brittle Bars

Preparation Time: 15 minutes
Cooking Time: 28 minutes
Servings: 5-6

## Recipe Ingredients:
**Ingredients:**
- 1-½ cups of all-purpose flour
- ½ cup of whole wheat flour
- 1 cup of packed brown sugar
- 1 teaspoon of baking soda
- ¼ teaspoon of salt
- 1 cup of butter

**Topping**
- 1 cup of milk chocolate chips
- 2 cups of salted peanuts
- 12¼ ounces of caramel ice cream topping
- 3 tablespoons of all-purpose flour

## Cooking Instruction:

1. At first, mix flours with salt, baking soda, and brown sugar in a large bowl. Spread the batter in a greased SearPlate.

2. Transfer the SearPlate to Ninja Foodi Dual Heat Air Fry Oven and close the door. Select "Bake" mode by rotating the dial.

3. Press the TIME/SLICES button and change the value to 12 minutes. Press the TEMP/SHADE button and change the value to 350°F.

4. Press Start/Stop to begin cooking. Spread chocolate chips and peanuts on top. Mix flour with caramels topping in a bowl and spread on top, Bake again for 16 minutes.

5. Serve.

# Cherry Jam tarts

Preparation Time: 15 minutes
Cooking Time: 40 minutes
Servings: 5-6

## Recipe Ingredients:
- 2 sheets shortcrust pastry

**For the frangipane**
- 4 ounces of butter softened
- 4 ounces of golden caster sugar
- 1 egg
- 1 tablespoon of plain flour
- 4 ounces of ground almonds
- 3 ounces of cherry jam

**For the icing**
- 1 cup of icing sugar
- 12 glacé cherries

## Cooking Instruction:

1. Grease the 12 cups of the muffin tray with butter, and roll the puff pastry into a 10 cm sheet, then cut 12 rounds out of it.

2. Place these rounds into each muffin cup and press them into these cups, and transfer the muffin tray to the refrigerator and leave it for 20 minutes.

3. Add dried beans or pulses into each tart crust to add weight. Transfer the muffin tray on wire rack in Ninja Foodi Dual Heat Air Fry Oven and close the door.

4. Select "Bake" mode by rotating the dial. Press the TIME/SLICES button and change the value to 10 minutes.

5. Press the TEMP/SHADE button and change the value to 350°F. Press Start/Stop to begin cooking.

6. Now remove the dried beans from the crust and bake again for 10 minutes in Ninja Foodi Dual Heat Air Fry Oven.

7. Meanwhile, prepare the filling beat, beat butter with sugar and egg until fluffy. Stir in flour and almonds ground, then mix well.

8. Divide this filling in the baked crusts and top them with a tablespoon of cherry jam. Now again, carefully place the muffin tray in Ninja Foodi Dual Heat Air Fry Oven.

9. While you continue cooking on the "Bake" mode for 20 minutes at 350°F. Next, whisk the icing sugar with 2 tablespoons water.

10. Top the baked tarts with sugar mixture.

11. Serve and enjoy!

# Cookie Cake

Preparation Time: 10 minutes
Cooking Time: 10 minutes
Servings: 1-2

## Recipe Ingredients:
- 1 stick butter, softened
- ½ cup of brown sugar, packed
- ¼ cup of sugar
- 1 egg
- 1 teaspoon of vanilla extract
- 1½ cups of all-purpose flour
- ½ teaspoon of baking soda
- 1 cup of semi-sweet chocolate chips

## Cooking Instruction:

1. Mix the cream, butter, brown sugar, and sugar in a large mixing bowl. Also mix in the vanilla and eggs until everything is well mixed.

2. Slowly stir in the flour, baking soda, and salt until combined, then stir in the chocolate chips.

3. Spray a 6-inch pan with oil, pour half of the batter into the pan, and press it down to evenly fill it. Refrigerate the other half for later use.

4. Place on wire rack inside the oven. Turn on Ninja Foodi Dual Heat Air Fry Oven and rotate the knob to select "Air Fry".

5. Select the timer for 5 minutes and the temperature for 370°F, remove it from the oven and set it aside for 5 minutes to cool.

# Fried Oreo

Preparation Time: 5 minutes
Cooking Time: 5 minutes
Servings: 7-8

## Recipe Ingredients:
- 8 Oreo cookies
- 1 package of Pillsbury crescents rolls

## Cooking Instruction:
1. On a cutting board or counter, spread out the crescent dough, then press down into each perforated line with your finger to make one large sheet.

2. Cut the dough into eighths. Meanwhile, in the center of each crescent roll square, place one Oreo cookie and roll each corner up.

3. Bunch up the remaining crescent roll to completely cover the Oreo cookie, and place the Oreos in an even row in the SearPlate.

4. Turn on Ninja Foodi Dual Heat Air Fry Oven and rotate the knob to select "Bake". Select the timer for 5 minutes and the temperature for 320°F.

5. Allow cooling for two minutes before serving.

# Chocolate Chip Cookies

Preparation Time: 10 minutes
Cooking Time: 45 minutes
Servings: 3-4

## Recipe Ingredients:
- ½ cup of butter, melted
- ¼ cup of packed brown sugar
- ¼ cup of granulated sugar
- 1 large egg
- 1 teaspoon of pure vanilla extract
- 1½ cups of all-purpose flour
- ½ teaspoon of baking soda
- ½ teaspoon of kosher salt
- ½ teaspoon of chocolate chips

## Cooking Instruction:
1. Whisk together melted butter and sugars in a medium mixing bowl. Whisk in the egg and vanilla extract until fully combined.

2. Combine the flour, baking soda, and salt. Scoop dough onto the SearPlate with a large cookie scoop (approximately 3 tablespoons), leaving 2 inches between each cookie, and press to flatten slightly.

3. Turn on Ninja Foodi Dual Heat Air Fry Oven and rotate the knob to select "Air Fry". Select the timer for 8 minutes and the temperature for 350°F.

4. When the unit beeps to signify it has preheated, open the oven door and insert the SearPlate in the oven.

5. Allow cooling for two minutes before serving.

# Banana Pancakes Dippers

Preparation Time: 10 minutes
Cooking Time: 15 minutes
Servings: 1-2

## Recipe Ingredients:
- 1½ cups of all-purpose flour
- 3 bananas, halved and sliced lengthwise
- 1 tablespoon of baking powder
- 1 tablespoon of packed brown sugar
- 1 teaspoon of salt
- ¾ cup of whole milk
- ½ cup of sour cream
- 2 large eggs
- 1 teaspoon of vanilla extract

## Cooking Instruction:
1. At first, combine flour, baking powder, brown sugar, and salt in bowl, then mix the milk and sour cream in a separate bowl, then add the eggs one at a time.

2. Pour in the vanilla extract. Combine the wet and dry ingredients until just mixed.

3. Next, grease the SearPlate with cooking spray and line it with parchment paper.

4. Place bananas on SearPlate in a single layer on parchment paper after dipping them in pancake batter.

5. Turn on Ninja Foodi Dual Heat Air Fry Oven and rotate the knob to select "Air Roast".

6. Select the timer for 16 minutes and the temperature to 375°F. Allow cooling for two minutes before serving.

# Cinnamon Rolls

Preparation Time: 5 minutes
Cooking Time: 30 minutes
Servings: 5-6

## Recipe Ingredients:
- 2 tablespoons of butter, melted
- 1/3 cup of packed brown sugar
- ½ teaspoon of ground cinnamon
- Salt, to taste
- All-purpose flour for surface
- 1 tube refrigerated crescent rolls
- 56g cream cheese, softened
- ½ cup of powdered sugar
- 1 tablespoon of whole milk

## Cooking Instruction:
1. Combine butter, brown sugar, cinnamon, and a large pinch of salt in a medium mixing bowl until smooth and fluffy.

2. Roll out crescent rolls in one piece on a lightly floured surface. Fold in half by pinching the seams together.

3. Make a medium rectangle out of the dough. Cover the dough with butter mixture, leaving a ¼-inch border.

4. Then roll the dough, starting at one edge and cutting crosswise into 6 pieces. Next, line bottom of air fry basket with parchment paper and brush with butter.

5. Once done, place the pieces cut-side up in the prepared air fry basket, equally spaced. Turn on Ninja Foodi Dual Heat Air Fry Oven and rotate the knob to select "Broil".

6. Select the timer for 15 minutes and the temperature for LO.

7. Allow cooling for two minutes before serving.

# Blueberry Hand Pies

**Preparation Time:** 15 minutes
**Cooking Time:** 20 minutes
**Servings:** 7-8

## Recipe Ingredients:
- 1 cup of blueberries
- 2½ tablespoons of caster sugar
- 1 teaspoon of lemon juice
- 1 pinch salt
- 320g refrigerated pie crust
- Water

## Cooking Instruction:
1. Combine the blueberries, sugar, lemon juice, and salt in a medium mixing bowl. Then, carefully roll out the piecrusts and cut out 6-8 separate circles (4 inches).

2. In the center of each circle, place roughly 1 spoonful of the blueberry filling. Wet the edges of the dough and fold it over the filling to create a half-moon shape.

3. Gently crimp the piecrust's edges together with a fork. Then, on the top of the hand pies, cut three slits.

4. Evenly, spray cooking oil over the hand pies, then place them onto the SearPlate. Turn on Ninja Foodi Dual Heat Air Fry Oven and rotate the knob to select "Bake".

5. Select the timer for 20 minutes and the temperature for 350°F. Once the unit beeps to signify it has preheated, open the oven door and insert the SearPlate in the oven.

6. Allow cooling for two minutes before serving.

# Broiled Bananas with Cream

Preparation Time: 5 minutes
Cooking Time: 10 minutes
Servings: 2-3

## Recipe Ingredients:
- 3 large bananas, ripe
- 2 tablespoons of dark brown sugar
- ⅔ cup of heavy cream
- 1 pinch flaky salt

## Cooking Instruction:
1. At first, slice the bananas thickly. Arrange in the SearPlate, gently overlapping.

2. Sprinkle the brown sugar evenly on top, followed by the cream and then the salt.

3. Turn on Ninja Foodi Dual Heat Air Fry Oven and rotate the knob to select "Broil".

4. Select the unit for 7 minutes at HI, and when the unit beeps to signify it has preheated, open the oven door and insert the SearPlate.

5. Close the oven and cook until the cream has thickened, browned, and become spotty.

6. Allow cooling for two minutes before serving.

## Roasted Bananas

**Preparation Time:** 5 minutes
**Cooking Time:** 7 minutes
Servings: 1-2

### Recipe Ingredients:
- 1 banana, sliced
- Avocado oil for cooking spray

### Cooking Instruction:
1. Using parchment paper, line the air fry basket. Place banana slices in the air fry basket, making sure they do not touch.

2. Mist banana slices with avocado oil, and turn on Ninja Foodi Dual Heat Air Fry Oven and rotate the knob to select "Air Roast".

3. Select the timer for 5 minutes and the temperature for 370°F, remove the banana slices from the basket and carefully flip them.

4. Cook for another 3 minutes, or until the banana slices are browning and caramelized. Remove from the basket with care.

5. Allow cooling for two minutes before serving.

# Chocolate Oatmeal Cookies

**Preparation Time:** 15 minutes
**Cooking Time:** 10 minutes
**Servings:** 35-36

## Recipe Ingredients:
- 3 cups of quick-cooking oatmeal
- 1½ cups of all-purpose flour
- ½ cup of cream
- ¼ cup of cocoa powder
- ¾ cup of white sugar
- 1 package instant chocolate pudding mix
- 1 teaspoon of baking soda
- 1 teaspoon of salt
- 1 cup of butter, softened
- ¾ cup of brown sugar
- 2 eggs
- 1 teaspoon of vanilla extract
- 2 cups of chocolate chips
- Cooking spray

## Cooking Instruction:
1. Start by using parchment paper, line the air fry basket, using nonstick cooking spray, coat the air fry basket.

2. Combine the oats, flour, cocoa powder, pudding mix, baking soda, and salt in a mixing dish. Set aside.

3. Mix cream, butter, brown sugar, and white sugar in a separate bowl using an electric mixer. Combine the eggs and vanilla essence in a mixing bowl.

4. Mix in the oatmeal mixture thoroughly, also mix the chocolate chips and walnuts in a bowl. Using a large cookie scoop, drop dough into the air fry basket; level out and leave about 1 inch between each cookie.

5. Turn on Ninja Foodi Dual Heat Air Fry Oven and rotate the knob to select "Air Fry". Select the timer for 10 minutes and the temperature for 350°F.

6. Before serving, cool on a wire rack.

# Cherry Clafoutis

Preparation Time: 15 minutes
Cooking Time: 25 minutes
Servings: 3-4

## Recipe Ingredients:
- 1½ cups of fresh cherries, pitted
- 3 tablespoons of vodka
- ¼ cup of flour
- 2 tablespoons of sugar
- Pinch of salt
- ½ cup of sour cream
- 1 egg
- 1 tablespoon of butter
- ¼ cup of powdered sugar

## Cooking Instruction:
1. In a bowl, mix together the cherries and vodka. In another bowl, mix together the flour, sugar, and salt.

2. Add the sour cream, and egg and mix until a smooth dough form. Grease a cake pan. Place flour mixture evenly into the prepared cake pan.

3. Spread cherry mixture over the dough. Place butter on top in the form of dots. Press AIR OVEN MODE button of Ninja Foodi Dual Heat Air Fry Oven and turn the dial to select "Air Fry" mode.

4. Press TIME/SLICES button and again turn the dial to set the cooking time to 25 minutes. Now push TEMP/SHADE button and rotate the dial to set the temperature at 355°F.

5. Press "Start/Stop" button to start. When the unit beeps to show that it is preheated, open the oven door, and arrange the pan on wire rack.

6. Insert in the oven. When cooking time is completed, open the oven door and place the pan onto a wire rack to cool for about 10-15 minutes before serving.

7. Now, invert the Clafoutis onto a platter and sprinkle with powdered sugar. Cut the Clafoutis into desired sized slices and serve warm.

# Vanilla Soufflé

Preparation Time: 15 minutes
Cooking Time: 23 minutes
Servings: 5-6

## Recipe Ingredients:
- ¼ cup of butter, softened
- ¼ cup of all-purpose flour
- ½ cup of plus 2 tablespoons sugar, divided
- 1 cup of milk
- 3 teaspoons of vanilla extract, divided
- 4 egg yolks
- 5 egg whites
- 1 teaspoon of cream of tartar
- 2 tablespoons of powdered sugar plus extra for dusting

## Cooking Instruction:
1. In a bowl, add the butter, and flour and mix thoroughly until a smooth paste form. In a medium pan, mix together ½ cup of sugar and milk over medium-low heat.

2. Cook for about 3 minutes or until the sugar is dissolved, stirring continuously. Add the flour mixture, whisking continuously and simmer for about 3-4 minutes or until mixture becomes thick.

3. Remove from the heat and stir in 1 teaspoon of vanilla extract. Set aside for about 10 minutes to cool.

4. In a bowl, add the egg yolks and 1 teaspoon of vanilla extract and mix well. Add the egg yolk mixture into milk mixture and mix until well combined.

5. In another bowl, add the egg whites, cream of tartar, remaining sugar, and vanilla extract and with a wire whisk, beat until stiff peaks form.

6. Fold the egg white mixture into milk mixture, and grease 6 ramekins and sprinkle each with a pinch of sugar.

7. Place mixture into the prepared ramekins and with the back of a spoon, smooth the top surface.

8. Press AIR OVEN MODE button of Ninja Foodi Dual Heat Air Fry Oven and turn the dial to select "Air Fry" mode.

9. Press TIME/SLICES button and again turn the dial to set the cooking time to 16 minutes. Now push TEMP/SHADE button and rotate the dial to set the temperature at 330°F. Press "Start/Stop" button to start.

10. When the unit beeps to show that it is preheated, open the oven door, and arrange the ramekins on wire rack and insert in the oven.

11. When cooking time is completed, open the oven door and place the ramekins onto a wire rack to cool slightly.

12. Sprinkle with the powdered sugar and serve warm

# Fudge Brownies

Preparation Time: 15 minutes
Cooking Time: 20 minutes
Servings: 7-8

## Recipe Ingredients:
- 1 cup of sugar
- ½ cup of butter, melted
- ½ cup of flour
- ⅓ cup of cocoa powder
- 1 teaspoon of baking powder
- 2 eggs
- 1 teaspoon of vanilla extract

## Cooking Instruction:
1. Start by greasing the SearPlate. In a large bowl, add the sugar and butter and whisk until light and fluffy.

2. Add the remaining ingredients and mix until well combined, then place mixture into the prepared pan and with the back of a spatula, smooth the top surface.

3. Press AIR OVEN MODE button of Ninja Foodi Dual Heat Air Fry Oven and turn the dial to select "Air Fry" mode.

4. Press TIME/SLICES button and again turn the dial to set the cooking time to 20 minutes.

5. Now push TEMP/SHADE button and rotate the dial to set the temperature at 350°F. Press "Start/Stop" button to start.

6. When the unit beeps to show that it is preheated, open the oven door. Insert the SearPlate in the oven.

7. When cooking time is completed, open the oven door and place the SearPlate onto a wire rack to cool completely.

8. Cut into 8 equal-sized squares and serve.

# Nutella Banana Muffins

Preparation Time: 15 minutes
Cooking Time: 25 minutes
Servings: 11-12

## Recipe Ingredients:
- 1⅔ cups of plain flour
- 1 teaspoon of baking soda
- 1 teaspoon of baking powder
- 1 teaspoon of ground cinnamon
- ¼ teaspoon of salt
- 4 ripe bananas, peeled and mashed
- 2 eggs
- ½ cup of brown sugar
- 1 teaspoon of vanilla essence
- 3 tablespoons of milk
- 1 tablespoon of Nutella
- ¼ cup walnuts

## Cooking Instruction:

1. Grease 12 muffin molds. Set aside. In a large bowl, put together the flour, baking soda, baking powder, cinnamon, and salt.

2. In another bowl, mix together the remaining ingredients except walnuts. Add the banana mixture into flour mixture and mix until just combined. Fold in the walnuts.

3. Place the mixture into the prepared muffin molds. Press AIR OVEN MODE button of Ninja Foodi Dual Heat Air Fry Oven and turn the dial to select "Air Fry" mode.

4. Press TIME/SLICES button and again turn the dial to set the cooking time to 25 minutes. Now push TEMP/SHADE button and rotate the dial to set the temperature at 250° F.

5. Press "Start/Stop" button to start. When the unit beeps to show that it is preheated, open the oven door.

6. Arrange the muffin molds on wire rack and insert in the oven, and when cooking time is completed, open the oven door.

7. Place the muffin molds on a wire rack to cool for about 10 minutes. Carefully, invert the muffins onto the wire rack to completely cool before serving.

# Air Fried Churros

Preparation Time: 15 minutes
Cooking Time: 12 minutes
Servings: 7-8

## Recipe Ingredients:
- 1 cup of water
- ⅓ cup of butter, cut into cubes
- 2 tablespoons of granulated sugar
- ¼ teaspoon of salt
- 1 cup of all-purpose flour
- 2 large eggs
- 1 teaspoon of vanilla extract
- oil spray

**Cinnamon Coating:**
- ½ cup of granulated sugar
- ¾ teaspoons of ground cinnamon

## Cooking Instruction:
1. Grease the SearPlate with cooking spray. Warm water with butter, salt, and sugar in a suitable saucepan until it boils.

2. Now reduce its heat, then slowly stir in flour and mix well until smooth. Remove the mixture from the heat and leave it for 4 minutes to cool.

3. Add vanilla extract and eggs, then beat the mixture until it comes together as a batter. Transfer this churro mixture to a piping bag with star-shaped tips.

4. Pipe the batter on the prepared SearPlate to get 4-inch churros using this batter. Refrigerate these churros for 1 hour, then transfer them to the Air fry sheet.

5. Transfer the SearPlate into Ninja Foodi Dual Heat Air Fry Oven and close the door. Select "Air Fry" mode by rotating the dial.

6. Press the TEMP/SHADE button and change the value to 375°F. Press the TIME/SLICES button and change the value to 12 minutes, then press Start/Stop to begin cooking.

7. Meanwhile, mix granulated sugar with cinnamon in a bowl. Drizzle this mixture over the air fried churros. Serve.

# Air Fried Doughnuts

Preparation Time: 15 minutes
Cooking Time: 6 minutes
Servings: 7-8

## Recipe Ingredients:
- Cooking spray
- ½ cup of milk
- ¼ cup/1 teaspoon of granulated sugar
- 2 ¼ teaspoons of active dry yeast
- 2 cups of all-purpose flour
- ½ teaspoon of kosher salt
- 4 tablespoons of melted butter
- 1 large egg
- 1 teaspoon of pure vanilla extract

## Cooking Instruction:
1. Warm up the milk in a suitable saucepan, then add yeast and 1 teaspoon of sugar, then mix well and leave this milk for 8 minutes.

2. Add flour, salt, butter, egg, vanilla, and ¼ cup of sugar to the warm milk. Mix well and knead over a floured surface until smooth.

3. Next, place this dough in a lightly greased bowl and brush it with cooking oil. Cover the prepared dough and leave it in a warm place for 1 hour.

4. Punch the raised dough, then roll into ½-inch-thick rectangle. Cut 3" circles out of this dough sheet using a biscuit cutter.

5. Now, cut the rounds from the center to make a hole. Place the doughnuts in the air fry basket. Transfer the basket to Ninja Foodi Dual Heat Air Fry Oven and close the door.

6. Select "Air Fry" mode by rotating the dial. Press the TIME/SLICES button and change the value to 6 minutes.

7. Press the TEMP/SHADE button and change the value to 375°F. Press Start/Stop to begin cooking. Cook the doughnuts in batches to avoid overcrowding.

8. Serve fresh.

# Cannoli

Preparation Time: 15 minutes
Cooking Time: 12 minutes
Servings: 11-12

## Recipe Ingredients:

**Filling**
- 1 (16-ounce) container ricotta
- ½ cup of mascarpone cheese
- ½ cup of powdered sugar, divided
- ¾ cup of heavy cream
- 1 teaspoon of vanilla extract
- 1 teaspoon of orange zest
- ¼ teaspoon of kosher salt
- ½ cup of mini chocolate chips, for garnish

**Shells:**
- 2 cups of all-purpose flour
- ¼ cup of granulated sugar
- 1 teaspoon of kosher salt
- ½ teaspoon of cinnamon
- 4 tablespoons of cold butter, cut into cubes
- 6 tablespoons of white wine
- 1 large egg
- 1 egg white for brushing
- Vegetable oil for frying

## Cooking Instruction:

1. For the filling, beat all the ingredients in a mixer and fold in whipped cream, then cover and refrigerate this filling for 1 hour.

2. Mix all the shell ingredients in a bowl until smooth. Cover this dough and refrigerate for 1 hour. Roll the prepared dough into a ⅛-inch-thick sheet.

3. Cut 4 small circles out of the prepared dough and wrap it around the cannoli molds. Brush the prepared dough with egg whites to seal the edges.

4. Place the shells in the air fry basket. Transfer the basket to Ninja Foodi Dual Heat Air Fry Oven and close the door.

5. Select "Air Fry" mode by rotating the dial. Press the TIME/SLICES button and change the value to 12 minutes.

6. Press the TEMP/SHADE button and change the value to 350 degrees F. Press Start/Stop to begin cooking.

7. Place filling in a pastry bag fitted with an open star tip. Pipe filling into shells, then dip ends in mini chocolate chips.

8. Transfer the prepared filling to a piping bag. Pipe the filling into the cannoli shells.

9. Serve and enjoy!